101 Things Great Dads Do

JAY PAYLEITNER

HARVEST HOUSE PUBLISHERS
EUGENE, OREGON

Cover design by Garborg Design Works

Cover photo © HalfPoint / Bigstock

Published in association with the Steve Laube Agency, LLC, 24 W. Camelback Rd. A-635, Phoenix, Arizona 85013.

Some material adapted from *The Dad Manifesto* (Harvest House, 2016).

101 Things Great Dads Do
Copyright © 2018 by Jay Payleitner
Published by Harvest House Publishers
Eugene, Oregon 97408
www.harvesthousepublishers.com

ISBN 978-0-7369-7399-1 (pbk.)
ISBN 978-0-7369-7400-4 (eBook)

Library of Congress Cataloging-in-Publication DataNames: Payleitner, Jay K., author.
Title: 101 things great dads do : small acts that make a big difference / Jay
    Payleitner.
Other titles: One hundre one things great dads do
Description: Eugene, Oregon : Harvest House Publishers, 2018.
Identifiers: LCCN 2017061382 (print) | LCCN 2018017298 (ebook) | ISBN
    9780736974004 (ebook) | ISBN 9780736973991 (paperback)
Subjects: LCSH: Fatherhood--Religious aspects--Christianity. | Child
    rearing--Religious aspects--Christianity. | Parenting--Religious
    aspects--Christianity. | BISAC: RELIGION / Christian Life / Men's Issues.
    | RELIGION / Christian Life / Family.
Classification: LCC BV4529.17 (ebook) | LCC BV4529.17 .P395 2018 (print) |
    DDC 248.8/421--dc23
LC record available at https://lccn.loc.gov/2017061382

Printed in the United States of America

18 19 20 21 22 23 24 25 26 / BP-SK / 10 9 8 7 6 5 4 3 2 1

"I've always loved Jay's take on fatherhood and recommend his stuff to my two married sons, each of whom is a father to four. *101 Things Great Dads Do* offers a lot more tools for your parenting utility belt."

—**Jerry B. Jenkins, bestselling author and coauthor of the *Left Behind* series**

"Dads are, quite simply, the most powerful force in the universe—just look at our heavenly Father. Dads have the power to create, energize, encourage, inspire, heal, correct, rescue, forgive, and teach unforgettable lessons. Jay Payleitner gives us 101 reminders of just how cool it is to be a dad."

—**Brett Clemmer, president and CEO, Man in the Mirror**

"Jay's book is inspiring and practical! If you want to be a great dad, you just found a jackpot of ideas that lead to connections that can make a lasting impact!"

—**David Horsager, bestselling author and CEO, Trust Edge Leadership Institute**

"Very few things exceed the importance and joy that come with being a dad. Jay's words offer crucial and practical insight, helping us firmly establish life lessons and create eternal memories with our children."

—**Matt Haviland, author of *A Father's Walk* and founder of A Father's Walk ministry**

"Jay has done it again! Every dad reading this book will realize we get only one chance as each year passes with our kids. Jay gives us 101 ways to have a lifelong influence."

—**Grady Hauser, speaker and author of *Passing the Baton***

"*101 Things Great Dads Do* makes fatherhood actionable. Written in the context of Scripture, it provides practical tips any dad can use to create emotionally and spiritually intimate relationships with his children."

—**Christopher Brown, president, National Fatherhood Initiative**

"There is no better gift for my three sons than *101 Things Great Dads Do*. Jay Payleitner writes from experience and from a commitment to help other dads enjoy the adventure of fatherhood."

—**Kendra Smiley, speaker and author of *Journey of a Strong-Willed Child***

"I want to be a great dad! My kids and my wife also want me to be a great dad. Sometimes I need ideas, inspiration, or simply a kick in the pants to be intentional in this role. Jay Payleitner gives me all of this and more in *101 Things Great Dads Do*. I look forward to telling other dads about this book and even giving copies to young dads."

—**Mike Young, founder of Noble Warriors and president of National Coalition of Ministries to Men**

"Jay's wonderful book reminds me of what my mother told me when I was ten years old, lying on a hillside on a cold November night, watching hundreds of shooting stars in the dark sky and drinking hot chocolate. Mom said, 'RJ, we are building memories.'"

—**RJ Fischer serves with The Navigators and Encore Ministries**

"As a fathering coach, Jay shares personal stories with tried-and-true action steps guaranteed to enhance the skill set of every man who is ready to be a great dad!"

—**Michelle Watson, author of *Dad, Here's What I Really Need from You***

"A boatload of great ideas that any dad can do with his children. Any book that devotes a whole chapter to giving noogies gets my Familyman Seal of Approval. This is one book you're going to want—not just on your library shelf but also in the bathroom, where you do your serious reading."

—**Todd Wilson, author, speaker, founder and host of familymanweb.com**

"With simple ideas that any dad can pull off, Jay shows us how every dad can truly be a great dad."

—**Todd Cartmell, author of *8 Simple Tools for Raising Great Kids***

"Jay Payleitner has created another valuable resource for all dads who want to be more intentional about their fathering. Children benefit dramatically when dads are present physically, emotionally, financially, and spiritually."

—**David Hirsch, founder, 21st Century Dads Foundation and Illinois Fatherhood Initiative**

To my dad,
my sons,
and my grandsons

Contents

Preface

I wrote this book just for you.

Of course, no two dads are alike. We all have different talents, experiences, foibles, and frustrations. But without a doubt, quite a few of these 101 ideas and strategies will apply *exactly* to your current life situation.

Especially if you're a dad with more than one kid, because each child is different and requires a unique combination of love, comfort, nudges, and connecting points.

Especially if you're a dad with pretty good kids, because you can't just go on cruise control when they're doing fine. You need to be intentional about pouring into their lives.

Especially if you're having a tough time connecting as a dad. These pages just might hold a single secret that makes all the difference in the world for your son or daughter.

Especially if you're a new dad. For obvious reasons, the earlier you start thinking about your role as a dad, the better.

Especially if you're an across-town dad, because you need to make the most of every minute you have with those kids you love so much.

Especially if you're a busy single dad, because there are shortcuts, hacks, and smiles in these pages you can use today. And mercifully, the chapters are short.

Especially if you're a granddad looking back on your days as a young father and wondering if you did okay. The answer is yes. Because all we can do is our best. Plus, you'll be reassured when you come across things you *did* do!

Since I began writing to dads more than a decade ago, several amazing and encouraging things have happened.

Statistically, fathers across the country are spending more time than ever with their children. Also, more organizations are making new efforts to encourage fathers in their journey.

Personally, I've had the privilege of speaking to thousands of men on the topic of fathering at Iron Sharpens Iron conferences and a variety of events sponsored by churches, businesses, service clubs, prisons, the Salvation Army, the US military, and others.

Beyond live speaking events, I've been interviewed on scores of radio and television programs on the topic of fatherhood and family relationships, including multiple appearances on *Focus on the Family*, *The Harvest Show*, and *100 Huntley Street*.

Perhaps most notably, since the release of my bestselling book *52 Things Kids Need from a Dad*, I've written more than a dozen books on family relationships with sales of more than half a million books.

Finally, I've watched three of my sons become dads. And that has been one of the most soul-satisfying experiences in my life.

My sons are great dads. In many ways, they don't need me anymore. At the same time, my grandkids have given me more reason than ever to live abundantly. Plus, watching my own sons and daughters-in-law, I am learning new strategies about the whys, hows, and wherefores of parenting.

This book is a culmination of all of the above. Talking with dads across the country during weekend events. Learning from other fathering experts at CoMission rallies. Testifying in Washington, DC at a summit on responsible fathering. Bonus insight from men who have overcome their struggles as fathers. Fresh lessons learned through my own growing family.

In these pages, we'll revisit and expand on some truths previously published. We'll apply some old truths to challenges your parents never faced, especially regarding technology and screen time.

These *101 Things Great Dads Do* are certainly not my last writing on the topic. But the book does cover just about everything I've uncovered over the years. Let's call it "the best of the best."

So. Dad. Get ready to do stuff that only you can do. Like skip rocks, chat over waffles, explain syzygy, be a sparring partner, do prayable moments, make stilts, laugh over spilled milk, splurge, and wake your kid for a lunar eclipse.

1

Stop and Catch the Fireflies

I thank my God every time I remember you.
PHILIPPIANS 1:3

A friend of mine told me his favorite memory growing up. He was eight or nine. His dad was a hardworking businessman. Three-piece suit. Wingtip shoes. Always coming or going on an important business trip. My friend vividly remembers driving with him on a two-lane country road at twilight. Suddenly, his father pulls off onto the shoulder and jumps out of the car. He opens the trunk, grabs a clean glass jar, and knocks on the passenger window, motioning his son to follow him out into the grassy field. To catch lightning bugs.

They poked some holes in the jar lid and threw in some grass. (Why do we do that?) They captured maybe six or eight of the flashing insects. Ten minutes later that father and son were back in the car with muddy sneakers and wingtips.

Please note, this wasn't a week at Disney World or a ski trip to Aspen. Still, that brief side-of-the-road adventure created a huge, lasting memory for my friend.

These days, entomologists tell us there are fewer fireflies. Conservationists would discourage us from interfering with the mating rituals of insects and, at the very least, practice catch and release. A child psychologist might suggest we not traumatize our children with spontaneous evening activities in unfamiliar locations.

Too bad. Because as we create this list of 101 things for great dads to do, this one might be at the very top. Take it literally. Or take it as a metaphor. Dad...stop and catch the fireflies.

2

Buy a Unicycle

Test everything; hold fast what is good.
1 THESSALONIANS 5:21 ESV

A unicycle is hanging in my garage. It's never been ridden. And that's okay.

We bought it for Randy's ninth birthday. He tried it. His brothers and sister tried it. Neighbors and friends tried it. It turns out that riding a unicycle is one of those things that requires a significant choice. A potential unicycle rider needs to either invest many, many hours…or not. A dad can't make that kind of decision. It's up to the individual.

Of course, you should never make your child feel bad for not achieving something that may not even be possible. You can't look at a boy or girl and tell whether they have the mental gyroscope required to balance and pedal a unicycle.

As a matter of fact, the chance that your child will master the one-wheeled beast is pretty slim. So why would I make such a suggestion? Because our job as dads is to open doors for our kids. To give them a chance to try new things. Art. Athletics. Music. Astronomy. Physics. Stand-up comedy. Poetry. Chess. Photography. Computer programming. Podcasting. Blogging. Culinary arts. Horseback riding. Spelunking. Storytelling. Pyrotechnics. Dance. Filmmaking. Or maybe unicycle riding.

If you see a spark of interest, invest a bit more time and money. Open the door a little wider and let your kids give their new hobby a try under your watchful guidance. Maybe right in your driveway. They may test it and say no thanks. Or they may master a new skill and run off and join the circus. Which, again, is really okay. Right?

3

Play Kick the Can, Red Rover, Spud, Dodgeball, Capture the Flag, or Hide-and-Seek

The city streets will be filled with boys and girls playing there.
ZECHARIAH 8:5

Want your kids to put down their screens? Well, you could yell at them: "Go outside and play!" That always works, right? You could bribe them with cash or baked goods. That's also probably not the best habit to get into. You could set up an intricate schedule for iPad, smartphone, and gaming device usage, exchanging chores for minutes and requiring them to be outside in the fresh air for 45 minutes for every hour of screen time. But who's really going to track that timetable?

A more viable alternative is to stimulate innovative outdoor activities. Anything to get them out into the sunshine, engage their imagination, or elevate their heart rate. Consider bubble wands, hula hoops, sidewalk chalk, a swing set, a wading pool, or a basketball hoop. Frisbees, Wiffle Balls, bikes, trikes, skateboards, street hockey goals and gear. Nerf toys, ring toss, squirt guns, water balloons, wagons, doll strollers, butterfly nets, a playhouse, a tree house, and so on. (Please don't turn them loose with lawn darts, hoverboards, or firecrackers.)

Toss a fresh can of tennis balls to your couch-potato kids. Sign them up for a charity bike ride or church-sponsored work crew to do chores for the elderly or shut-ins. See what the local park district offers for the upcoming season. Anything to get them to stop staring at screens, right?

Well, how about this? The best replacement for screen time is dad time. Whatever game you played as a kid, teach it to *your* kids. And the *neighborhood* kids. Join the fun. Just make sure you're on the winning team.

Repeat after me, "Olly olly oxen free!" Or something like that.

4

Trigger Traditions

So then, brothers, stand firm and hold to the traditions that you
were taught by us, either by our spoken word or by our letter.
2 THESSALONIANS 2:15 ESV

As kids get older, you'll experience busy seasons of life during which family members head off in all different directions. One of God's great inventions for reuniting scattered families is the tradition. You can usually count on the youngest members of your family to remember traditions. But it's pretty much up to Dad to keep them. You're the one who sees the bigger picture and has the authority to put everything else on hold and make sure the family comes together to do something "we always do."

Of course, as the calendar turns, holidays bring their own traditions. Easter egg hunts. Your favorite spot for watching fireworks. Visiting the same pumpkin patch year after year. Green bean casserole. Neighborhood caroling.

Then there's an entire array of traditions that are not on your calendar, but happen anyway. You don't even have to think about them, and they require no preparation. You know the triggers:

- The first nice weekend of summer triggers a family bike ride.
- The first snowfall of the year that has "good packing" triggers a family snowman contest. (Or snowball fight.)
- Your local high school presents their annual musical, so you order tickets for the Sunday matinee.
- The park district holds a ribbon cutting at a new

playground, and your kids are first in line to try the new curvy slide and climbing ropes.

- Shamrock Shakes come out at McDonald's, so you make a family dessert run.

- The church across town holds their live nativity scene, so you bundle up the kids and go.

- The zoo announces a new baby giraffe or lion cub, which means your family will be one of the first in line to see the little cutie.

Hot-air balloon launches, classic car shows, harvest festivals, music performances in the park, homecoming football games, and other activities that show up in the local newspaper or social media feed all might fall into this category.

As hard as you might try, I'm not sure even a great dad can orchestrate these kinds of family traditions. True traditions evolve spontaneously. So be warned. To a kid, if you do something just twice, they expect it to become a time-honored, unwritten law set in stone. As my daughter, Rae Anne, said years ago insisting we stop for cones at an ice-cream store near the bike trail, "We have to stop here. It's a tradition!" And, you know what? We had stopped there only two other times, but she was absolutely right.

Give Noogies

God decided in advance to adopt us into his own family
by bringing us to himself through Jesus Christ. This is what
he wanted to do, and it gave him great pleasure.
EPHESIANS 1:5 NLT

One of the great privileges of fatherhood is roughhousing a bit with the kids. The joy of being a dad should overflow into making physical connections with sons and daughters at every age and stage.

When they're babies, burble their tummies and squeeze their toes. Toddlers need to be rassled and tumbled. Horseyback rides work too. During grade school, make sure they get an equal dose of hugs, tickles, and noogies. That leads right into other physical contact as they mature, including dancing with your daughter and modeling a good, firm, respectful handshake. For the record, all kids—if they choose—should be able to sit in their dad's lap anytime.

Noogies, tickles, and tummy burbles can be grand traditions to begin each day, to welcome Daddy home, or at bedtime. Ask four-year-olds if they've had their noogies today. If they say no, then you have the responsibility to rescue them from their noogie-less condition. If they say yes, then you have two choices. Give them an advance dose of noogies for tomorrow. Or simply say, "Thank goodness, because I'm all out. Do you have any noogies you can spare?" Then watch out.

When it comes to noogies, bear hugs, and so on, we're not talking about abuse. Just the opposite! As a matter of fact, healthy physical contact between dads and kids helps build protection against unhealthy physical contact with those who might harm your precious kids.

6

Teach Stuff Before
They Learn It in School

Walk with the wise and become wise,
for a companion of fools suffers harm.
PROVERBS 13:20

Want to set your child up for success in the classroom? It's easier than you think. Find out what your school district is teaching your kids a year from now, and *you* teach it to them now. Suddenly—before anyone else in the class—your son or daughter has a head start on topics like opposites, multiplication, centripetal force, the three states of matter, the seven continents, suffixes and prefixes, adjectives and adverbs, the Magna Carta, the Mason-Dixon Line, photosynthesis, Venn diagrams, and anything else you come up with that might be on the school district syllabus for the upcoming year.

Moms have been doing this for years. They get their preschoolers ready for kindergarten by teaching them numbers, colors, animal names, and even some phonics. But after formal education begins, most parents lose track of what's coming up in the next school year. Rather than anticipating, parents simply respond to the daily homework that the entire class is doing.

I know this idea is a bit of a con game. Your kid may or may not actually be any smarter than the other kids. But really, isn't this just another way of helping your child become a lifelong learner? And it's not a bad thing if their teacher and the classmates look at your son or daughter as a leader and scholar. Everyone in that classroom—including your own child—will have heightened expectations for their performance.

Funny thing about expectations. They tend to come true.

Laugh with Them. Cry with Them.

Rejoice with those who rejoice,
and weep with those who weep.

ROMANS 12:15 NASB

When our kids come to us with emotional news, why do we often reflect the opposite emotion back to them?

I will never forget a brief conversation I had with my dad my junior year of high school after showing him my first-place trophy for a junior varsity wrestling tournament. Of course, being on a JV team as a junior is not exactly impressive, and the trophy was only about four inches tall. Still, I had beat every other wrestler in my bracket, and a brief celebration of my modest achievement seemed appropriate.

My dad looked at the trophy and said, "Maybe next year you can win a varsity trophy." Ouch. Of course, he meant it as a challenge to keep working hard and reach for the stars. But at that moment, his words cut me like a knife. They took the joy out of the day's victory.

In other scenarios, it's easy to imagine a child sharing some disappointing news and a father dismissing the child's grief or frustration. Your daughter loses the student body election, and you respond by telling her that student council is a joke and a waste of time. Or your son doesn't make the show choir, and you say something about how he should be going out for football anyway. Does that sound like you? When your kids are hurting, are you sometimes oblivious?

When any member of your family comes to you revealing a clear emotion, remember Romans 12:15. It's a great teaching—especially appropriate for dads—on how to respond to almost any emotion. Simply reflect their demeanor right back to them. In the moment, celebrate with them in their joy or join them in their sorrow. Use phrases like, "That's fantastic" or "Oh, man, I'm so sorry."

Other examples are easy to come up with. When your college-bound kid proudly shows you a letter of acceptance from the local state college, please don't express disappointment because you were hoping the letter was from your alma mater or an Ivy League school.

When your third-grader comes to you in tears because her best friend, Zoe, is moving to another state, your first response should be, "Oh, I'm so sorry, sweetie." Give her a hug and let her cry for a moment. Only then have you earned the right to offer a bit of wisdom and perspective. "I'll bet it will be hard for Zoe too. Maybe we can pray that she makes some new friends at her new school." Or, "Should we have a going-away party for her?" Or maybe, "Now you have a friend in Idaho! That's kind of cool."

Dad, in the moment, match their emotion. Rejoice with them. Weep with them. Don't throw cold water on their successes. And don't minimize their grief. Later on you can guide, offer other options, or inspire them to the next level of achievement.

8

Don't Curse the Train, Count the Train Cars

Dear brothers and sisters, when troubles of any kind come your way, consider it an opportunity for great joy. For you know that when your faith is tested, your endurance has a chance to grow. So let it grow, for when your endurance is fully developed, you will be perfect and complete, needing nothing.

JAMES 1:2-4 NLT

Yes, freight trains are frustrating. But while you're muttering under your breath, what is that eight-year-old in the backseat doing? He is gleefully counting the cars! Even worse, when the number reaches 70 or so, he begins to hope for 100!

Here's an idea, Dad. Model patience. Especially in those critical years when your son or daughter is watching your every move, look at any trouble or inconvenience as a way to demonstrate that you trust God. Model to your children how minor irritations are gifts that allow our endurance to grow. It's all good, because God is in control of everything.

As the saying goes, "When life gives you lemons, make lemonade." How? When it comes to exasperating railroad crossings, let those train cars trigger a dialogue with your young passenger.

Topics might include imagining what that train might be carrying or where it might be headed. Contemplate why railroad tracks must be parallel. Define parallel. Have a discussion about Bernoulli's principle, the golden spike that completed the first transcontinental railroad in Utah in 1869, why train graffiti is both an art form and a crime, or why going around railroad gates is an extremely bad idea.

Or you could simply count the cars.

9

Spy on Your Kids

I urge you, brothers and sisters, to watch out for those who cause divisions and put obstacles in your way that are contrary to the teaching you have learned. Keep away from them.

ROMANS 16:17

You need to know stuff about your kids they don't know you know. One more time. You need to know stuff about your kids they don't know you know. Here's how.

Network with other parents. We have a saying in our house: "Our spies are everywhere." It sounds like a joke, but it's not. We know hundreds of parents, and they know our kids. I'm not saying "it takes a village to raise a child." Raising our children is a job for which my wife and I take full responsibility, but it's still a blessing to have other parents in the neighborhood, on the sidelines, in the auditorium, and just living life in our hometown who know and care about our kids.

Be tech savvy. You don't have to have multiple accounts on every social media site, but stay connected with parents and other individuals who are in the know and in the loop. If it makes sense, take advantage of the latest technology to know the location of cars and cell phones. Expect that sometime, somewhere, your teenager is going to be at a gathering where something dangerous or illegal is going down. When a situation comes to your attention, don't overreact. Don't accuse. Your child may be totally innocent, but you have the right and responsibility to get the facts.

Consume what they consume. Read some of the stuff they read. Watch some of the stuff they watch. Listen to some of the stuff they listen to. Play some of the games they play. You may fall asleep at the formulaic animated features. You may roll your eyes at the simplistic teen-angst comedies. You may be disturbed by suggestive music lyrics or the graphic nature of some popular movies or television shows. You may get angry at some of the worldview opinions expressed in the stuff they read. But as you immerse yourself in their culture, you'll know more about your kids. A word of caution: Don't automatically assume your kids endorse or mimic everything they watch, read, or hear. As they sample culture, they, like you, will consider, judge, and accept or reject what's offered.

I'm not suggesting you should sneak into your teenagers' rooms and read their diaries. But absolutely be aware of the world in which they live. Your goal is not to bust them for minor bad decisions. Your goal is to know who they are and how they see themselves so that you can protect them and help them reach their full potential.

They trust you to not embarrass them or be a snoop. But they also trust you to do whatever it takes to protect them from evil. If you have hard evidence that your kid is making choices that threaten their well-being, then take action. Whatever it takes.

10

Snuggle

"For I know the plans I have for you," declares the Lord,
*"plans to prosper you and not to harm you, plans
to give you hope and a future."*
JEREMIAH 29:11

I'm here to confirm that this one-word snippet might be the most critical thing that a dad might do.

Snuggling is a lost art. Our schedules are too crowded. Our lives are too separate. Our hands are too full of screens, phones, and remotes. And for some people—men especially—there may be a bit of hesitation about getting too close and holding on too long. But let me confirm that snuggling matters. It literally saves lives. I've seen it firsthand.

My wife, Rita, likes to hold babies, and babies like to be held. As a result, over a period of several years, we welcomed ten foster babies into our home. Mostly newborns. Some had been exposed to cocaine in their mother's womb, which meant these babies were essentially recovering addicts. I will never forget watching Rita and my five kids hold those precious infants while they endured seizures and severe withdrawal tremors.

The good news is that love is the most powerful force in the universe. Snuggles from my family literally loved the residual cocaine right out of those babies. The boys and girls we've been able to keep track of over the years are doing very, very well.

Which brings us back to the value of snuggling. If snuggling can heal a newborn suffering from nine months of fetal cocaine exposure, then imagine what snuggling does for healthy babies! And school-age kids. And tweens. And teens. And adult children.

Are you with me? If you're still a snuggle naysayer, a definition might help. Snuggling with our kids describes close, intimate moments of discovery, whispering, plotting, and dreaming. With a newborn, it's a swaddle. As they get older, the place and relationship evolves. Sitting close on a couch watching old movies. In a cozy corner reading a picture book. On a log watching a dancing campfire. At bedtime with moonbeams streaming in the window.

Now of course, moms typically are better snugglers than dads. Moms tend to be a little softer and often have the benefit of breast-feeding, which is an entirely unique form of snuggling. All of which means dads have to be even more intentional about plopping on a couch, putting an arm around a shoulder, or making their lap available.

During a good snuggle, you and your child—at any age—are establishing a pattern of trust and communication. You'll want to be especially aware of a critical turning point right around second or third grade. At that moment, you may be tempted to give up on snuggling, but please don't! That's when they need you to stay close and be available because that's when make-believe begins to morph into reality. That's when your child will first start to think, *Maybe I can be anything; maybe God has a special plan for me, and maybe I can make a difference in this world.*

In the same way, for older kids, the security generated from snuggling gives them the confidence to believe they can make it on their own in college, the military, or the working world.

11

Respect Their Mom

A wife of noble character who can find? She is worth far more than rubies. Her husband has full confidence in her and lacks nothing of value. She brings him good, not harm, all the days of her life.
PROVERBS 31:10-12

I have a fantastic wife. If it weren't for Rita, I would be living in a van down by the river. She's easy to love and has earned my respect and admiration.

Honestly, I don't know what it's like to be in long-term conflict with my wife. I don't know what it's like to be separated or divorced, scraping up child support, agonizing over my inability to see my kids, and wondering why I'm not living happily ever after. If that describes your life, my heart aches for you and your entire family.

Dad, if you've been through a divorce, you have some extra work to do. At some point, you may want to acknowledge your share of the responsibility for past mistakes. Make extra effort to be respectful of your children's mom. Treat her with dignity. Refrain from shouting, blaming, or name-calling. Respond to her requests, keep the lines of communication open, and work things out in a way that is as fair as possible to all parties involved.

Respect, common courtesy, and communication are not just priorities for single dads. That's the bare minimum for any husband.

If you are fortunate enough to have a longtime partner in this adventure of parenting, let her know how much you appreciate what she means to you and the kids. Never ever take your bride for granted.

12

Quit Smoking

He must manage his own family well and see that his children
obey him, and he must do so in a manner worthy of full respect.
1 TIMOTHY 3:4

You can't tell your kids to not smoke if you smoke. Well, actually you can, but it will have little impact. One thing kids can spot a mile away is a hypocrite. Especially in a dad trying to wield a hollow hammer of self-righteousness or enforce discipline only when he feels like it.

You're not one of *those* dads, are you? The kind that curses, frequents every tavern in town, and mocks religion. Then he acts surprised and blames someone or something else when his kid's life is marked by profanity, overindulgence, and godlessness.

Of course you're not that dad. But what are you modeling to the next generation?

Children who endure ongoing criticism will learn to malign others. Young people who are conditioned to disrespect authority will never trust a teacher, pastor, or boss who probably has their best interest in mind. Kids who live without any approval or praise will never be confident enough to try new things. Kids who watch Dad mope and whine will be mopers and whiners.

Conversely, dads who demonstrate integrity, respect, self-discipline, generosity, and gentleness have a better chance of raising kids with those same worthwhile traits.

So imagine the character traits you wish for your kids as they reach adulthood. Then live them.

Go the Extra Mile

Love each other with genuine affection,
and take delight in honoring each other.
ROMANS 12:10 NLT

With our Boy Scout troop, my brother, Mark, and I made a two-day, 35-mile journey down the Fox River from Yorkville to Ottawa, Illinois, where it empties into the Illinois River. The first morning, my dad drove his two sons down to the canoe launch, made sure our life vests were snug, and waved goodbye as more than two dozen scouts paddled down the mighty Fox. Moving with the current, even the novice paddlers got into a nice rhythm and were making good time. This wasn't exactly a wilderness adventure; we would pass homes, factories, dams, and overpasses along the way.

A mile or two into our journey, the canoes approached a bridge spanning the river. Standing right in the middle of the overpass was our dad. While the other mothers and fathers had left the launch site and headed back to their other obligations for the day, Ken Payleitner had chosen to make one more connection with his two sons. Mark and I were surprised and delighted to see him. He didn't shout instructions or embarrass us. Instead he just waved as our canoes passed beneath the concrete overpass. Why was he there? Maybe he wanted to make sure we were safe. Maybe he was relieving his guilt for not volunteering to be one of the adult supervisors. Maybe he just wanted to connect with his boys. In any case, it was a nice touch.

Then things began to get interesting. Several miles later, Dad was at the next overpass. And the next. And the next. I don't remember how much time elapsed between bridges. I don't know how fast he drove to get to the next bridge or how long he waited. And I don't remember exactly how many bridges he was on. But it began to be a game. Our canoes would round a bend in the river, we'd spot an overpass in the distance, and a handful of scouts would strain to see if Mr. Payleitner was waiting. There he was. As for me, I was glad that much-heralded figure was my dad.

Of course, there was a bit of a disappointment when we finally came to a bridge on which he was not waiting. That's the risk when you start playing that kind of game. But I'm glad that didn't keep my dad from playing. His entire investment was probably a couple hours and a quarter tank of gas. Clearly it was worth it.

As I write this 40 years later, I realize my dad frequently and intentionally created those small moments of connection with his sons. Through modeling, he taught me to do the same. I also came to realize fathering is not about showing up at graduations, orchestra concerts, championship games, award ceremonies, and canoe launches. That's the bare minimum. We need to invest in our kids *between* those milestones. Dad, commit to going the extra mile.

14

Laugh over Spilled Milk

Fathers, do not exasperate your children;
instead, bring them up in the training and instruction of the Lord.
EPHESIANS 6:4

Accidents happen. Your young son or daughter already feels bad for spilling their milk. Why do we pile on? Yelling at them will not improve the situation. Yelling will only exasperate your kids. When the milk glass tumbles, your best course of action is to throw napkins at the spill and keep repeating, "No problem. No problem."

After all, when you brought that little one home from the hospital, you were agreeing to clean up a certain number of milk spills over the next decade or so. It's truly inevitable.

Once you've solved the immediate crisis, you have a chance to assess the next course of action. Maybe your milk glasses need to be easier to grip. Maybe you pour smaller portions for a while. Without too much fanfare, keep a roll of paper towels within reach. But please don't make your eight-year-old revert to using a sippy cup.

An excellent dad response would be to recall embarrassing moments in your own life, when you dipped your tie into the gravy boat or tucked the tablecloth into your pants and pulled the entire table setting onto your lap. Make something up if you have to—the more outlandish the better. Then, with an understanding smile, thank them in advance for being extra careful. That lesson just may stick.

If your child does something naughty with intent and maliciousness, that's another story. But accidents happen. Dad, you can set the tone for your kids to learn from their mistakes.

Respond to Any Crisis, "I Love You. It Will Be Okay. We'll Get Through This Together."

The righteous cry out, and the LORD hears them;
he delivers them from all their troubles.
The LORD is close to the brokenhearted
and saves those who are crushed in spirit.

PSALM 34:17-18

When bad stuff happens to your kids, you want them to come to you. Believe it or not, you want that phone call. "Dad, I wrecked the car." "Dad, I'm dropping out of school." "Dad, I'm in jail." "Dad, I'm pregnant." "Dad, my girlfriend is pregnant."

Those things are not good news, of course. But those cries for help are signs that you're doing something right. You have earned their trust. You have established yourself as a hero who delivers unconditional love.

Kids of any age need to be able to pick up their cell phone and call Dad. When you get that call, be thankful. They could have called someone else, but they knew you would rise to the occasion and be the dad.

They also know there will still be consequences. They're not "off the hook." Maybe later you will deliver a short lecture, insist on an apology, or require some financial restitution, but for now you are the one individual they can count on. You will be the voice of reason. You will help sort out the stuff that matters from the stuff that doesn't. You will protect them from further harm. Their trustworthy dad will help them see the big picture and move forward with hope and confidence. Plus, you will make sure the punishment fits the crime.

Be aware, this understanding and trust needs to be established early. When you step on a Lego, when they leave the milk out overnight, when they lose the TV remote...please don't overreact. In the grand scheme of things, those things are not a big deal. As they get older, the challenges get bigger. Way bigger.

When they're three or seven or twelve or nineteen and they mess up, you need to be able to calmly say, "I love you. It'll be okay. We'll get through this together." Say it out loud, even now. That needs to be the attitude of your heart and the understanding of your children.

Dad, life will hit the fan. When it does, you want your kids coming to you, because the world does not love them. The world is broken. And the world will give them bad advice.

By the way, when God looks at the mess-ups of each of us believers, he says the same thing. "I love you. It will be okay. We'll get through this together."

Tuck In

My son, do not let wisdom and understanding out of your sight,
preserve sound judgment and discretion...
When you lie down, you will not be afraid;
when you lie down, your sleep will be sweet.

PROVERBS 3:21,24

Dad, if you're not tucking your kids in at night, you're missing out. It's the absolutely best time to enter their world and really get to know what's on their hearts and minds. The lights are dim. The house is quiet. Prayers are said. The crud of life melts away. Words of love and encouragement come easily.

When you tuck in, you get a chance to put perspective on whatever happened that day—the small victories, questions that came up, and any frustrations that still linger. You find out about the bully or the new friend. You deliver simple truths or sort out the grand puzzles of life. There in the quiet, it's much easier for a dad to make his kids feel safe enough to reveal their fears and their aspirations. You're setting the tone for the next day and ensuring their dreams will be sweet.

With a little perseverance, a father can develop a bedtime ritual that continues until the day you drop them off at their college dorm, give them one last hug as they join the armed forces, or celebrate a new season of life as they move into their own place. Over those two decades or so, the schedule will change, the topics of discussion will surely evolve, and you will miss a night or two. The experience itself may include book reading, stuffed-animal chatting, day reviewing, memory sharing, and adventure planning.

Eventually, you'll probably stop calling it "tucking in." But if you are tenacious about spending time every night with your kids, you will build a connection that will lead to rewarding moments of affection and insight, as well as opportunities to walk your children through challenges and heartaches of life.

Plus, while Dad is tucking in the kids, Mom gets a few minutes at the end of the day to breathe and reboot. That's a gift she will certainly appreciate. When Dad finally slips out of the child's bedroom, there's a good chance that Mom will be ready for some grown-up conversation or other activities that never happen when the kids are around.

Make tucking in a habit when they're young, and you'll be welcome in your child's room every night for 18 years or more. Some nights it might be just two minutes. Some midnight conversations with an older teen might go for hours.

Start when they're about a year and a half old. Or start tonight. Tucking in may be the best investment of your time you'll ever make.

17

Say Bedtime Prayers

Therefore let us draw near with confidence to the throne of grace, so that we may receive mercy and find grace to help in time of need.

HEBREWS 4:16 NASB

There are 650 prayers listed in the Bible.[1] Jesus is recorded praying 25 times. The apostle Paul instructs his new converts, "Pray without ceasing" (1 Thessalonians 5:17 NASB). Prayer is clearly important.

But the most important thing you need to know about prayer is this: The Creator of the universe desperately wants to hear from you and from the child you love so much. Just before lights-out is a great time to come together and pray. For sure, keep praying at meals, as you travel, in every crisis, and at special occasions. But I urge you, Dad, to take full advantage of bedtime prayers.

Bedtime prayer should be a routine. But the prayer itself is not routine at all. As you dim the lights and tuck in, see if you can find a new reason each night to give glory, give thanks, and ask for God's intervention. Tell your children that God already knows their every need but still loves to hear their heartfelt words. And please don't include any of that "if I should die before I wake" imagery.

When they're little, keep it short and sweet. Nothing scary or ominous. As they get older, stretch those prayers. Go a bit longer. Pray for events and people outside your family. Add your own personal concerns. Encourage them to add their own voice. Maybe even keep a prayer log to record answered prayer. You may be surprised by many of the gratifying answers to your children's sincere, trusting prayers.

18

Rake Leaves Together

Two are better than one,
because they have a good return for their labor.
ECCLESIASTES 4:9

Chores, by definition, require a young person to personally commit to a task and see it through to the end. Pretty much by themselves. But some tasks—although they may be hard work and eat up an entire Saturday—are better suited for two or more members of the family. Those multi-person chores can take on an entirely different tone. I recommend you make the most of it.

Specifically, we're talking about things like planting a garden, cleaning the garage, reorganizing the basement or attic, shoveling snow, mending fences, putting up Christmas decorations, and the ultimate autumn family chore: raking leaves.

If you live someplace where raking leaves isn't required because of your living accommodations, lack of trees, or tropical climate, then I feel a little sorry for you. Swooshing leaves into a pile, dragging them to the curb, and—if it's legal—burning your colorful collection is a tradition every kid should experience. Typically, the weather is cool. You pull out your favorite sweatshirts and directly participate in the magical change of seasons. The crunch of fallen leaves underfoot and the crisp autumn air assault the senses. And what's more fun than jumping in a huge pile of orange, red, and purple leaves?

Jobs you do together should never feel like punishments. Think of it as family teamwork. Make sure every member pitches in with assignments that fit their skill level—just challenging enough. When the task is complete, high fives all around!

The family that sweats together, sticks together. You can quote me on that.

Stop Raking to Watch the Geese Fly South in V Formation

*Look at the birds of the air; they do not sow or reap or
store away in barns, and yet your heavenly Father feeds
them. Are you not much more valuable than they?*

MATTHEW 6:26

S ome of the greatest joys of working together as a family happen
when the work stops. For a well-earned break. For lunch. Because
the sun is setting. Or because the job is finished. Applause and
appreciation all around.

The best kind of break happens naturally, triggered by a spontaneous occurrence. For example, geese flying south. Stop when you hear
the honking. Talk about why some animals migrate. Ask your kids
why geese fly in a V formation. It's okay if they don't know. Even orni-
thologists disagree, offering two possible explanations. One is to con-
serve energy by taking advantage of the upwash vortex fields created
by the lead bird's wings. The other possible explanation is that the V
angle facilitates orientation and communication among the flock. In
any case, chatting about geese is a good excuse for taking a rake break.

In the same way, you'll want to take snow-shoveling breaks to make
snow angels, car-washing breaks to have a water fight, and attic-cleaning
breaks to share memories triggered by any box marked "keepsakes."

Now, as a bonus, one of my favorite jokes. Practice it and have it
ready next time your family is raking leaves together: "Hey, kids. Scien-
tists just discovered why—when geese fly overhead in a V formation—
one side of the V is longer than the other one. Do you know why?"

"Umm, no. Why?"

"Because it has more geese in it."

Ignore the Stickball Dents on the Garage Door

Fools vent their anger,
but the wise quietly hold it back.
PROVERBS 29:11 NLT

When I pulled up to my driveway, I saw it instantly. My son Isaac and his three college buddies had gashed my new $1,200 garage door playing stickball. Now, I knew my boys played driveway stickball. That's why I spent $1,200 on the heavy-duty garage door—one that would not be dented by plastic Wiffle Balls. Unfortunately, what I had not anticipated was that occasionally one of the batters might gash my new $1,200 garage door with that wooden broom handle on the backswing.

Did I mention the garage door cost $1,200?

So, here's the big question: How did I, as a father, react to those fresh dents in my fresh garage door? Actually, I did pretty well. My mind quickly calculated the value of the events taking place that afternoon in my very own driveway, and knew I had come out way ahead. My teenage son and some of his lifelong friends had chosen to hang out in my front yard. No beer cans were littering the front lawn. No police squad cars were pulling up with bad news. No creepy, dark video games were crashing and slashing in a dark basement. These young men were playing the time-honored game of stickball in the Payleitner driveway. What kind of investment does that require? Broom handle: $3. Wiffle Balls: $6. A garage door with stickball bruises: priceless. (Marked down from $1,200.)

I confess, at another time or place, I might have raged. But this time, reason prevailed. Somehow God helped me see the beauty of the moment. Instead of pointing out how Isaac had let me down, I had the good sense to smile and say, "Swing away." My son and his friends were wonderfully relieved.

Dad, I pray you have the same loving response when your door is dented. Otherwise, your son's pals might not feel welcome in your home. Even your own son might not feel welcome. And that would be tragic.

A home is to be lived in. If you stress out every time a floor gets scuffed, a table gets scratched, or a door gets dented, your home is not going to be a place where young people want to hang out. Make kids feel comfortable in your home, and you'll always know where your own kids are and who they're with.

Harmon Killebrew, the all-star power hitter for the Minnesota Twins, tells a great story:

> My father used to play with my brother and me in the yard.
>
> Mother would come out and say, "You're tearing up the grass."
>
> "We're not raising grass," Dad would reply. "We're raising boys."

Make Stilts

*The LORD makes firm the steps
of the one who delights in him;
though he may stumble, he will not fall,
for the LORD upholds him with his hand.*

PSALM 37:23-24

Got a free Saturday afternoon? Instead of watching golf or NAS-CAR for three hours, invest that time in your grade-school son or daughter. Even if you don't have an organized workshop, you can slap a few pieces of wood together, right? Don't make a birdhouse that sits passively waiting for a new tenant. Don't make some knick-knack that just sits on a shelf.

Search online for "homemade wooden stilts," and you'll find dad-friendly instructions with helpful illustrations. Or make a trip to the library and head straight for 684.08 in the Dewey Decimal System.

Each stilt is actually just two pieces of wood. The long piece could be a two-by-two about six or seven feet long. The other piece is the footrest. A triangle cut out of a scrap of two-by-four works well. Slap 'em together with screws, bolts, or even nails, and you're done. If you're an experienced carpenter, you're probably two steps ahead of me. Just remember not to leave your son or daughter behind. (This is quality time with your kid, okay?) If you're confused, that's also okay. Take the time to do the research and sketch it out.

Even without a fancy workshop, this shouldn't be an all-day project. Once you get the materials gathered from your scrap wood or local home center, it should come together pretty easily. On that first pair of stilts, you'll want to keep the footrests low—about a foot off the ground. You can always make a more challenging pair later.

Finally, how about a quick stilt-walking lesson? The key is to start with the poles under your armpits, straight out, as if you were jousting. You'll be tempted to hold them like ski poles, but that's not proper stilt-walking technique. To control them, you have to hunch over a little and wrap your arms around the poles and hold them with your thumbs pointing down. For a visual reference, again, you may want to head to the internet.

So get to it, Dad. Remember, this really isn't about researching, designing, shopping, sawing, nailing, drilling, sanding, screwing, or stilt-walking. It's about you and them. It's about living life and learning stuff together along the way. Don't worry if the quality of construction is not up to union standards. Don't worry if you bend a nail, drill a few extra holes, or skin a knee falling on the driveway. Don't worry if your kids are better stilt walkers than you. At this kind of stuff, all of my kids are better than me.

Oh yeah…when they do get that twelve-inch boost, suddenly your grade-schooler will be looking you right in the eye. That glimpse into the future makes the whole afternoon worthwhile.

22

See Your Kids as Future Adults

Be on guard; then you will not be carried away by the errors of these wicked people and lose your own secure footing. Rather, you must grow in the grace and knowledge of our Lord and Savior Jesus Christ.
2 PETER 3:17-18 NLT

Our kids are kids. And we need to accept the idea that they will make mistakes. They will fail. They will fall. For years, they are going to need our help, guidance, and supervision.

However, we also need to see them as future adults. When they stumble, we need to choose our response carefully. Sometimes we rescue. Sometimes we allow them to suffer minor consequences. Sometime we simply let them hit bottom and work it out for themselves. As our sons and daughters grow in wisdom and stature, we fathers should take great joy when our kids face a dilemma, consider their options carefully, and make adult decisions.

Absolutely, we should help them find and establish secure footing. Then we have to step back and let them deal with the victories and the setbacks. Those wins and losses will be relational, physical, educational, emotional, and spiritual. The world will continue to try to knock them off balance, but if their foundation is built with godly principles, they will keep their balance.

So next time you're wondering whether all the stuff you do as a dad is worth the effort, take a moment to stand back and see your son or daughter as a future adult. You may have to squint and use your imagination, but keep looking. The real deal is closer than you think.

Quit Golf

For everything there is a season,
and a time for every matter under heaven.
ECCLESIASTES 3:1 ESV

I love coaching baseball and softball at the level when young athletes first begin to understand the concept of force plays, tagging up, and looking for a good pitch to hit. That's about eight or nine years old. I coached teams for all five of my kids at that age.

One year, there was a young boy on our team who started slow but was improving by leaps and bounds. Unfortunately, his dad never saw him play. Our games were on weeknights, and that father had to travel Monday through Friday for work. (That happens sometimes and can't be avoided. I get that.)

When a rainout was rescheduled for Saturday, the boy was delighted. "Coach Payleitner, my dad can see me play!" I also was delighted and decided to let the young man show off for his dad. I'd start him at shortstop and bat him second in the lineup. Saturday morning, the young man comes hanging his head. He tells me, "My dad…can't come. He…has to play golf."

I was angry. The boy was broken. That father did not know how important his presence was to his son.

I can't say why that father chose golf over his son. But I can say, "Dad, for a season of life, make your kids your hobby." If they're into dinosaurs, American Girl, or skateboarding, you be into dinosaurs, American Girl, and skateboarding.

For a few critical years, set aside your own desires, distractions, and hobbies on their behalf. Maybe even quit golf.

24

Patiently Teach Them to Play Golf

Control your temper, for anger labels you a fool.
ECCLESIASTES 7:9 NLT

The last chapter suggested you quit golf. Well, here's a better idea. Commit yourself to a double dose of patience and invite your eight-, nine-, or ten-year-old to play nine holes with you this weekend. Or at least share a bucket of balls with them at the local driving range.

Much of what your son or daughter knows about competition, sportsmanship, and learning from failure is going to come from you, Dad. The best chance they have to come away with a wonderfully positive approach is by competing right alongside you. Right? Or is that a bad idea?

I'm not sure how your golf game is. And if you don't play golf, you may apply this principle to any favorite sport or competition. (Anything from video games to beanbag toss to Settlers of Catan.) But please consider this short chapter as a recommendation and a challenge to involve your son or daughter in your favorite hobby and make sure they see you *at your best*. Even if you double-bogey your way around the course.

Your best, of course, has nothing to do with your scorecard. Your best has everything to do with playing, competing, and learning together. And maybe even enjoying each other's company.

My wish for you is that you impress your child by hitting several solid drives and sinking a few 15-foot putts. But—and here's the point—I hope you impress them even more by smiling through your typical shanks, slices, and sand traps.

Who knows where that early golfing experience may lead your youngster? Of course, golf has all kinds of pitfalls beyond potential anger issues. Way too many golfers spend way too much time and cash that they could invest elsewhere. Also, please don't make the mistake of burdening your young golfer with dreams of the PGA tour. (Unless they're really, really good.) Most importantly, don't let your wife be a golf widow or the rest of your kids feel left out.

Still, I can certainly imagine several memorable moments that would be a welcome result of a father-son or father-daughter golfing hobby. The first time they make par on a hole. Their first birdie. The first time they make par on the front or back nine. The first time they beat you. And 20 years from now when you get a phone call…"Hey, Dad, want to play a round of golf this weekend?"

Sound good? Just remember, Dad, you could mess up that entire scenario by putting too much pressure on yourself or too much pressure on your son or daughter. Fore!

Teach Rock/Paper/Scissors

*A youngster's heart is filled with foolishness,
but physical discipline will drive it far away.*

PROVERBS 22:15 NLT

The random act of throwing a clenched fist, a flat palm, or a sideways peace sign gives any child a rare chance to beat their father fair and square.

But be warned. Teach a four-year-old to play rock/paper/scissors, and it will soon be a favorite pastime. You need to be prepared to play anytime and anywhere. It's actually a nice distraction when you're in line at an event, waiting for the gates to open. It's also one of those things that gives you a chance to say, "Hey, we've played a dozen games or so. Let's take a break."

The most important truth about rock/paper/scissors is a secret you must never share with your child. Here it is. When a new round begins, every kid between the age of four and nine will start by throwing "scissors." Guaranteed. Which means, if they need some cheering up or you want to give them a momentary thrill of victory, throw "paper." On the other hand—no pun intended—if you feel like flexing your superiority or you are deciding who should go do a minor chore, go ahead and throw "rock." You win, and they have to fetch the newspaper or empty the kitchen trash. Go ahead and try it out today. And please don't reveal this secret.

Tell Knock-Knock Jokes

The father of godly children has cause for joy.
What a pleasure to have children who are wise.
PROVERBS 23:24 NLT

Knock, knock. *Who's there?* Isabel. *Isabel who?* Isabel working? I had to knock.

Knock, knock. *Who's there?* Dwayne. *Dwayne who?* Dwayne the bathtub; I'm dwowning.

Knock, knock. *Who's there?* Orange. *Orange who?* Orange you going to answer the door?

Knock, knock. *Who's there?* Lettuce. *Lettuce who?* Lettuce in, it's cold out here.

Knock, knock. *Who's there?* Someone who can't reach the doorbell.

Knock, knock. *Who's there?* Radio. *Radio who?* Radio not, here I come.

Knock, knock. *Who's there?* Justin. *Justin who?* Justin the neighborhood and thought I'd drop by.

Knock, knock. *Who's there?* Ben. *Ben who?* Been knocking for 20 minutes!

Knock, knock. *Who's there?* Who. *Who who?* Nice owl. Do you do any other bird impressions?

Knock, knock. *Who's there?* Wooden shoe. *Wooden shoe who?* Wooden shoe like to know?

Knock, knock. *Who's there?* Hatch. *Hatch who?* Gesundheit.

Knock, knock. *Who's there?* Cows go. *Cows go who?* No, silly, cows go moo.

Knock, knock. *Who's there?* Little old lady. *Little old lady who?* Wow! I didn't know you could yodel.

Knock, knock. *Who's there?* Hanna. *Hanna who?* (singing) Hanna partridge in a pear tree.

Knock, knock. *Who's there?* Annie. *Annie who?* (singing) Annie thing you can do, I can do better...

Knock, knock. *Who's there?* Tank. *Tank who?* You're welcome.

Knock, knock. *Who's there?* Boo. *Boo who?* Well, it's only a joke. You don't have to cry about it.

Give Horsey Rides

For where your treasure is, there your heart will be also.
MATTHEW 6:21

If you can swing it financially, you'll probably want to take your family to Walt Disney World at least once. For the right age, the Magic Kingdom is indeed almost magic. But if you're talking about driving across several states or jumping on a plane with a three- or four-year-old, I'm not so sure.

Sure, you can plop a preschool child in a teacup, and they may enjoy flying on Dumbo. They will recognize Mickey, several princesses, and the Pixar characters. But when their tummy gets woozy and their attitude gets cranky, you'll be cutting short your big-ticket day at the park to head back to the overpriced hotel room. So my recommendation is to save the cash-grabbing theme parks for slightly older kids.

Instead, Dad, as your little ones transition from toddler to kindergartner, designate *yourself* as their favorite amusement park ride. Hoist them on your shoulders. Twirl them like a Tilt-A-Whirl. Let them dance on your shoes. And don't forget good ol' fashioned horsey rides. Practice your neighs. Teach your little cowpoke to say giddyap. Do a little bucking bronco. Let them feed you carrots.

Save your money. Invest your heart. Just don't toss them too high in the air. Hey, how often can you say that being a dad just saved you about $2,000?

Play H-O-R-S-E

As iron sharpens iron,
so one person sharpens another.
PROVERBS 27:17

You know how to play H-O-R-S-E, right? It's a driveway basketball game in which players take turns making similar shots. An easy layup. A hook shot from six feet out. A swish from the oil spot by the garage door. If you make it and the next player doesn't, he or she gets a letter. A player who gets five letters is eliminated. You can have a quick game with any number of players.

H-O-R-S-E works because it's just competitive enough. No one is dripping sweat, sucking wind, or throwing elbows. Breaks in the action can be filled with easygoing chatter and maybe even catching up on what's going on in the life of your young athlete. Plus, you get a chance to model the difference between respectful trash talk and the kind that is just plain mean.

So next time your son or daughter is out shooting around, put on your sneakers and trot out to the driveway, schoolyard, or playground. Meaningful conversations take place when a father and child are burning a little energy and shooting hoops. Same thing goes for batting cages, goalie practice, pickle (aka rundown, hot box, or running bases), monkey in the middle, running pass routes, and any other sporting endeavor in which you can still keep up with your son or daughter.

And again, keep the trash talk to a minimum.

Don't Let Them Win. They'll Beat You Fair and Square Soon Enough.

The godly walk with integrity;
blessed are their children who follow them.
PROVERBS 20:7 NLT

Never let your ten-year-old son or daughter beat you in drive-way basketball. Or checkers. Or Scrabble. Or Ping-Pong. Or anything that requires skill, knowledge, and practice. Because in just a few years, they will beat you. And that victory will be ever so sweet because it was earned.

There are exceptions to this rule. For example, go ahead and allow your preschooler to tackle you in knee football or pin you to the carpet in family-room wrestling. They know without a doubt that Daddy is bigger and stronger.

Allow your middle schooler to beat you in most video games. They will anyway, so don't kill yourself trying to be competitive. Their reflexes are faster, and they know shortcuts and secrets you don't.

Finally, you do have permission to intentionally lose a game of driveway basketball *under very specific conditions*. Let's say a young man has been working tremendously hard to improve his game. His father is still taller and stronger, but their games have been getting significantly more competitive. One night after dinner, that dad may want to go 90 percent and maybe even bank a couple close shots off the rim just to give his son a taste of victory. The lessons Dad teaches that night are about the value of hard work and how to lose graciously. If you try this, Dad, never let him know you threw the game, and make sure you beat him soundly the next few rounds. After that taste of victory over Dad, he'll work even harder on his game.

Kiss Your Wife in the Kitchen

Enjoy life with your wife, whom you love.
ECCLESIASTES 9:9

With marriages breaking up all around them, your kids need to know that Mom and Dad are committed to each other and that a long and happy marriage is worth fighting for.

That's right, your marriage matters to your kids. A recent study reveals that children of divorce are roughly twice as likely to see their own marriage end in divorce.[2] Conversely, any married couple that goes the distance literally increases the chances that their children will also have long, successful marriages.

Plus, you'll be helping your children avoid other well-documented, devastating effects of divorce on families:

- Children of divorced parents are roughly twice as likely to drop out of high school.[3]

- Children of divorce are at a greater risk to experience injury, asthma, headaches, and speech defects.[4]

- Teenagers in single-parent families and in blended families are three times more likely to need psychological help.[5]

- Seventy percent of long-term prison inmates grew up in broken homes.[6]

Of course, these are not absolutes, so please don't take anything for granted. But these stats do make you consider that there's some value in the concept of working on your marriage and staying together for the sake of the kids.

By the way, I'm not saying marriage is easy. It takes commitment, patience, sacrifice, and creativity. But that's also not to say marriage is a grueling marathon of misery. Proverbs 5:18-19 suggests that a long marriage could be a joyride. "Rejoice in the wife of your youth…May you always be captivated by her love" (NLT).

Raising expectations and finding joy in the marriage relationship are two things great dads do.

Now, I realize you may have been through divorce, custody battles, a second marriage, and other relational challenges. No two families are alike. I refer you back to chapter 11, "Respect Their Mom."

But if you are living under the same roof as your bride and your kids, I submit that one of the best fathering tips in the world can also be quite pleasurable: Kiss your wife in the kitchen.

It achieves three worthy objectives. It tells your bride you love her. It tells your kids you love their mom. It demonstrates to your kids that passion can happen in a committed, lifelong marriage relationship.

So go ahead and make out with your wife right there in the busiest room in the house. The goal is for your fourth grader to go "Ewwww!" or your teenager to wisecrack, "Get a room!" That's a sure signal you're doing it right.

Don't Be the Jerk in the Stands

*Everyone should be quick to listen, slow to speak and
slow to become angry, because human anger does
not produce the righteousness that God desires.*
JAMES 1:19-20

I am actually better than I was years ago, but over the years I did more than my share of stomping around sidelines, muttering under my breath, yelling at umpires and referees, and embarrassing my wife and kids.

Looking back, I can't bear to think of the way I acted. It's more than a little frustrating. It felt beyond my control, although that is certainly no excuse. The lowest point came when Max told me that if I didn't stop, he didn't want me to come to any more baseball games. That was a turning point for me. Until that moment, I wasn't sure my kids even heard my comments from the bleachers. Let me assure you, they did. And your kids hear yours.

So consider this your wake-up call to minimize or eliminate your jerk-in-the-stands behavior. If you have the courage, ask your kids if you've been a little too enthusiastic as a fan. Be ready to apologize and take steps to alleviate the problem.

Give your wife permission to give you a nudge if she senses your frustration building. Walk down to the end zone or foul pole. Give yourself a distraction. Volunteer to keep score, work the concession stand, video the action, work the chain gang at a football game, or be a linesman for soccer. Think about your witness as a Christian to other fans in the bleachers.

Or maybe pray away that demon and enjoy the game. What a concept.

Chaperone a School Dance

*When [Jesus's] parents saw him, they were astonished. His mother
said to him, "Son, why have you treated us like this? Your father and
I have been anxiously searching for you." "Why were you searching
for me?" he asked. "Didn't you know I had to be in my Father's
house?" But they did not understand what he was saying to them.
Then he went down to Nazareth with them and was obedient to
them. But his mother treasured all these things in her heart. And
Jesus grew in wisdom and stature, and in favor with God and man.*

LUKE 2:48-52

This passage from Luke is really the only time in the Bible that we
get a glimpse of Jesus during his formative years. Of course, the
entire passage is really all about revealing that Jesus's adult life will
focus on doing the will of the Father. But if you read between the lines,
there's also quite a bit of insight here for parents as well.

First, you shouldn't feel guilty for losing track of your 12-year-old.
Second, moms and dads sometimes miscommunicate. Third, there will
come a time when you will have to let go of your son or daughter and
let them find their way in this world. Fourth, sometimes kids need to
do their own thing without Mom or Dad hanging around.

Dad, all those solid lessons are based on the idea that as young people mature, they are practicing the skill of being separate from Mom
and Dad. Nevertheless, I recommend signing up to chaperone an occasional school dance, church event, or fund-raiser.

Initially, your middle schooler or high schooler may not be happy
about that. But if you stay in your assigned zone and don't embarrass
them, they'll actually be glad you're there. Don't expect to spend very
much time with your own child—if any. Their friends will probably

come over to say hi, but your own flesh and blood will stay far, far away. Just before the evening ends, your kid may stop by out of some sense of duty. That visit will include minimal conversation and no new information. Still, just by being there you'll pick up all kinds of insight into their world. The next day, just don't ask things like "Who was that couple dressed so silly, and what was that dance they were doing?"

Also, make sure you give your young social butterfly plenty of notice:

"The O'Briens asked us to help out at the Christmas dance. I guess we're in charge of the punch bowl."

"Just letting you know, I'm driving one of the vans for the weekend retreat. And I'm staying in the boys' cabin."

"Your mom and I are going to be checking in runners for the fun run next month."

One final note: Just do this. Go ahead and sign up. Don't ask your child's permission ahead of time. For obvious reasons, they'll say no. And really, can you blame them?

Earn the Right to Say
What Needs to Be Said

Don't get involved in foolish, ignorant arguments that only start
fights. A servant of the Lord must not quarrel but must be kind to
everyone, be able to teach, and be patient with difficult people.
Gently instruct those who oppose the truth. Perhaps God will
change those people's hearts, and they will learn the truth.

2 TIMOTHY 2:23-25 NLT

The title of "father" doesn't automatically mean your kids will listen to you. A dad can't demand respect; he can only earn it.

If you have a history of verbally trashing them or physically abusing them, what makes you think they will listen to anything you have to say? They won't.

Thankfully, the opposite is also true. If your verbal interaction is affirming and if your touch is always under control, you will be trustworthy. If you speak truth and listen to their side of the story before judging, your word has value. If you respond calmly and consistently to their tantrums, pouting, or whining, they will acknowledge you as a peacekeeper. If you listen to their fears and dreams without derision, they will seek out your wisdom and experience with confidence.

Where do you fall on this fathering spectrum? Can you be trusted? Do you bring peace to stormy conversations, or do you stir up more strife?

If you're just now realizing you may have lost some of your children's respect, you have some extra work to do. Begin today. Start with delivering your own heartfelt doses of love and respect. Use gentle words. Take time. Be patient.

Yes, truth needs to be spoken. But love first. And think about this:

Is what you are about to say true? Is it necessary? Is it helpful? Are you pulling your kids toward you or pushing them away?

Again, are you demanding respect or earning it?

How do kids respond to a father they respect? With obedience, affection, attention to what he has to say, confidence he will do his best, and trust that he will supply their needs.

Best of all, they will put down their phones, turn off the TV, take out their earbuds, or stop texting long enough to hold a real conversation.

Way too many dads lose their children's respect. When that happens, the life-changing conversations we want to have with our kids will never take place.

Your best chance at getting and keeping their respect is to start early. Up through the age of seven or eight, your son or daughter will give you plenty of opportunities to prove yourself to be reliable, compassionate, patient, and trustworthy. After that, it gets harder. Still, no matter what, don't give up.

Your kids are counting on you to say what needs to be said. As a great dad, you'll want to do everything you can to earn that right.

34

Chat over Waffles

*These commandments that I give you today are to be on
your hearts. Impress them on your children. Talk about
them when you sit at home and when you walk along
the road, when you lie down and when you get up.*

DEUTERONOMY 6:6-7

You know things your kids need to know. You've learned lessons your kids need to learn. If you can save them from making some of the same mistakes you made, that's not a bad thing. They also have questions, concerns, dreams, discoveries, fears, and ideas you need to know about. All this fascinating information cannot possibly be exchanged in a single speech or even a long weekend. You need to *do life* with your kids.

Especially as they get older, you'll want to intentionally create environments and situations that bring you face-to-face or side by side. Working. Traveling. Playing. Golfing. Competing. Gardening. Woodworking. Barbecuing. Stargazing. Dancing. Dining. Going out for ice cream. Strolling a beach. Shopping for a Mother's Day present. Or serving dinner in a homeless shelter. You get the idea.

Dad, feel free to interpret the above passage from Deuteronomy to suggest, "Talk to your kids about stuff that matters during TV commercials, riding in the car, strolling down a dirt road, when you're tucking them in bed, or at your favorite diner munching on blueberry waffles."

Do life together, and spontaneously the lines of communication will open and all those difficult and embarrassing lessons you learned over the years will finally make sense. Miraculously, you will have a chance to enlighten those little people you love so much with your hard-earned wisdom.

Survive the Asparagus Standoff

If you are willing and obedient,
you will eat the good things of the land.
ISAIAH 1:19

Choose your battles with your kids carefully, Dad. When you do choose one, try to win it. If it turns out to be unwinnable or ends in a stalemate, don't dwell on it. And avoid choosing that same battle until a new season of life comes around.

Battles you can win involve specific, reachable goals that can be monitored by Mom and Dad. The expectation or goal should be indisputably clear and grow out of logical reasoning. When the battle is over, any consequences should not be severe, oppressive, or impossible to enforce.

Winnable battles include things like these:

- "Put your stuffed animals in the basket, and then we can go to the park."
- "Wear a life jacket in the canoe."
- "No phones at the dinner table."

Examples of battles you might not win include...

- "Clean your room before you go to school."
- "Use your phone for emergencies only."
- "If you leave your bike in the rain, you can't ride it for a month."

These battles are unwinnable because you and your child may not agree on the definition of clean, emergencies, and rain. Plus, they're still going to school even if the room isn't clean. And a summer month without a bike is a long time.

Which brings me to the asparagus standoff—part of Payleitner family folklore.

Our kids were not fussy eaters. But one of them really didn't like asparagus. Actually, none of the kids liked asparagus.

During one particular dinner, one particular kid let it be known there was no way he was going to eat his asparagus. In my fatherly wisdom, I let it be known that he was not going to leave the dinner table without eating that asparagus—all four spears. It was a classic dinner-table standoff. Only one winner would emerge.

Truth be told, I like asparagus when it's grilled, buttered, and still hot. But as you'll probably agree, cold and mushy asparagus is sure to trigger a gag reflex. And that's exactly what the young diner did. He sat there several minutes, gave me the evil eye for several more, and finally shoved two or three cold, soggy asparagus spears into his mouth—gagging, choking, and spitting a few chunks of green goo back onto his plate.

The incident ended with an uncertain and hollow victory. I may have said something like, "Yes, you may be excused," pretending to maintain some semblance of parental control. The standoff was over. But I think I learned a greater lesson than my son did that evening.

I quietly suggested to Rita that we avoid serving asparagus for a while. We didn't tell that to the kids, but it just seemed like a battle we didn't want to fight again for a few months. And that was that.

The lasting impact of the event is really the most amusing part of the story. As adults, all our children enjoy fresh asparagus, especially grilled with garlic butter and fresh ground pepper, even ordering it in restaurants. When the plates are presented, one of the kids always says in mock seriousness, "No one leaves this table until you finish your asparagus."

Measure Their Growth

Like newborn babies, crave pure spiritual milk,
so that by it you may grow up in your salvation.
1 PETER 2:2

I n my youth, our family spent almost every Christmas Eve in the basement rec room of a favorite aunt and uncle. One of our annual traditions was marking the heights of all the cousins in pencil on the stud wall behind the basement door.

It really is an eye-opening moment when a child realizes he has literally grown in the last year. I remember stretching myself up so the pencil mark would be as high as possible. The archive of lines accompanied by names and dates was proof I had grown physically from Christmas Eve to Christmas Eve.

My aunt would always make a fuss about how much we had grown. I remember also how the pencil marks on the stud wall annually confirmed that I was not catching up with my brother Mark and probably never would.

But grow in wisdom and stature I did. Not as tall as I would have liked. Not as wise either. Any physical growth stopped decades ago. As for wisdom, I'll let you decide for yourself.

Dad, as the years go by, make sure your kids receive plenty of nourishment and physical exercise to grow in stature. That's something you can actually measure. And I absolutely recommend you mark their growth on a stud wall once a year. But make sure they also grow in wisdom. That's not as easy to quantify, so you'll have to stay close and see how they're progressing each and every season.

Do Sundays

Remember the Sabbath day, to keep it holy.
EXODUS 20:8 NASB

Do the Ten Commandments still have anything to say to us today? I think so. Unfortunately, our culture seems to be tossing them aside without much thought.

One lovely commandment that comes to mind is honoring the Sabbath. That idea is pretty much defunct, and most busy families are going along without any pushback at all.

How about your family? Is Sunday just like any other day? Sure, you try to round up the troops for church in the morning, but even that isn't an absolute priority. Then, once you're home, the day is a total free-for-all.

Sunday has become a convenient day to run to the mall or grocery store. To pay bills. Catch up on some work. Hunker down with your computer. For many families, Sunday is the busiest traveling sports day of the week, with tournaments from dawn to dusk.

A little work on Sunday is probably okay. But I hate that all the stores and quite a few offices and service centers are expected to be open on Sundays. That recent practice definitely steals family time. Sure, we want our teenagers to get part-time jobs, but that often means working weekends. Dads and moms are also clocking in on Sundays. It's not easy.

You know I'm not advocating sitting motionless from midnight to midnight. As a matter of fact, I'm hoping you'll become proactive scheduling family outings and projects. Raking leaves or washing the car with your eight-year-old might be exactly the right way to spend a pleasant Sunday afternoon. Proofreading your teenager's term paper that's due the next day is a really good idea. If you have a hobby you enjoy—even if it makes a little extra spending money—you should probably feel free to do that "work." If you can get the kids involved in a non-sweatshop kind of way, that's a win.

If you've read this far, I think we're probably in agreement. As a culture, we've lost some of the simple charms of what Sunday could and should be. Family time. Drinking lemonade on the porch. Picnics. Getting together with cousins and neighbors. Sunday drives out into the country. Dare I suggest that Sundays might be set aside for some spiritual reflection or family devotions?

For me, I confess that Sunday evenings often find me planning my upcoming workweek. And that's a shame. Sunday evenings are the exact time I should be investing in my family and helping them plan not just a week, but their lives.

Dad, how does your family do Sundays? Is an adjustment necessary?

Skip Rocks

*Whatever you do, whether in word or deed, do it all in the name
of the Lord Jesus, giving thanks to God the Father through him.*
COLOSSIANS 3:17

id your father teach you this critical life skill? Remember choosing just the right stone? Flat, but not too thin. Just the right circumference that it fits comfortably in the crook of your fingers. With just enough weight that it skips and doesn't plop into the water. Then leaning low and aiming your throw parallel to the surface of the pond or creek. Letting it fly. Part throw, part flip.

Three skips was a good start. But soon anything less than five skips was a fail. And you know what? It's perfectly okay for a dad to say, "Pretty good. Let's see if you can get six or seven now." No one's feelings get hurt even if the kids max out at five skips.

Skipping stones is a microcosm of the father-child relationship. In just 15 minutes, you present a new and challenging opportunity, let them try it on their own, allow them to fail, help them improve, and try again.

If you never skipped rocks with your father, that doesn't mean you're out of the loop here. I imagine you picked up the skill somewhere along the way. And if you're not adept at rock skipping, turn this idea into something you can learn right alongside your son or daughter.

No matter what, skipping rocks allows you to practice every teaching skill in the book. Words. Choice. Touch. Demonstration. Correction. Patience. Practice. Competition. Cheers.

By the way, this all takes place outside. Dads and kids today need more time outside.

Display Their Artwork
on the Refrigerator

He has filled them with skill to do all kinds of work as engravers,
designers, embroiderers in blue, purple and scarlet yarn and fine
linen, and weavers—all of them skilled workers and designers.

EXODUS 35:35

When your four-year-old proudly presents you with a drawing of what looks like a baboon wearing a babushka boiling boomerangs on a beach, you have two choices. You can crush their creative spirit, or you can catapult them into a world of imagination and innovation that will serve them well in all their endeavors for the rest of their lives.

Your first fatherly response to their fantastical drawing is obvious. You *oooh* and *aaah*. But after that, you need to be a little more calculated with your response. Your next goal is to find out what is actually *in* the drawing without letting them know you don't know.

Don't say, "What is it?" Instead, invite the young artist up on your lap and say, "Wow. This is most excellent. Tell me about it." Then start picking up on their verbal cues. Ask them open-ended questions that get them thinking and explaining. "How did you choose these two colors?" "These lines are straight and these are curvy. Why did you choose that?" The idea is to partner with them in the discovery of their own creative abilities and help them see how they have control over the creative choices they make.

You can point out elements of their artwork that are bold and decisive, even suggesting their efforts have led you to think new thoughts. Let them know that like all great works of art, their masterpiece has given you a new perspective on life, the world, or some other grand concept.

After your creative critique that is almost 100 percent positive, there's one more critical element of this conversation. You need to bring it to a satisfying closure. The best way to establish value to any artistic endeavor is to give it relevance, appreciation…and a permanent home. Ask your budding Picasso if you can keep this work of art. Of course, they will glow with pride and say yes.

Then, make a point to display it proudly on the wall, family bulletin board, or refrigerator. Let it hang on public display for all to see and admire. After a suitable amount of time, dethrone the drawing from its posting, write the child's name and date on the back in pencil, and slip the artwork into a memory box you keep for treasures like this.

Once in a while, sift through that box and marvel at how far your young artist has come. Feel free to take some of the credit because at that critical moment when they were four years old, you invested five minutes to appreciate their work.

40

Always Have a Clean Handkerchief

Praise be to the God and Father of our Lord Jesus Christ, the
Father of compassion and the God of all comfort, who comforts
us in all our troubles, so that we can comfort those in any
trouble with the comfort we ourselves receive from God.

2 CORINTHIANS 1:3-4

Mom's purse should always have hand sanitizer, rubber bands, nail clippers, matches, breath mints, a small sewing kit, Band-Aids, tissues, something to write with, something to write on, and something to help a headache.

Dad needs a clean hankie.

Perhaps it's a throwback to the days when gallant men offered their handkerchief to a lady who may be tearing up because that's what ladies do when they are extremely happy or extremely sad. Hankies also come in handy for a myriad of other manly reasons. As a tourniquet to stop severe bleeding. To clean spectacles. To dry your hands when today's loud, air-blowing hand dryers fail. To mop your brow after performing manly duties out in the sun. To blow your nose. And if absolutely necessary, to signal surrender to an enemy.

Handkerchief etiquette suggests you keep it folded into a neat square and offer it for comfort or cleaning only if it's still pristine. Never ask for it back, even if it's monogrammed. At weddings and funerals, especially, you may want to have more than one stashed in suit coat pockets. Dads should be vigilant, ever ready to come to the rescue with a handkerchief and a shoulder on which to cry. That's one more thing great dads do.

Volunteer at Their Stuff

As we have opportunity, let us do good to all people,
especially to those who belong to the family of believers.
GALATIANS 6:10

When it comes to strategies for how to get involved in your child's school, clubs, or church activities, here's a great hint for dads: Do what moms do.

For generations, moms have been showing up at elementary schools to help at holiday classroom parties, chaperone field trips to local museums, and serve as lunchroom helpers and playground monitors. Well, step up, Dad!

It's no longer unimaginable for fathers to volunteer at an elementary school, but kids still react with delight when a dad walks in a classroom or strolls the playground. The national organization WATCH D.O.G.S. (Dads of Great Students) even has a program for men to sign up to spend one day each school year at their child's school. You can be the hero of the hallway.

Churches are always looking for adult volunteers for their kids' programs and youth activities. Especially godly men. A call to the right staff person will get instant attention. After an interview and perhaps a background check, they'll put you right to work. You might monitor hallways and direct traffic. You might have direct interaction with kids. You could be a referee, speaker, group leader, or director. Or just a babysitter. I've done all of these things with no regrets.

I honor men and women who volunteer their time out of a selfless desire to pour into the lives of young people in the community. But my motivation was almost always selfish. I wanted to be in the same building with my sons or daughter. In many cases, I wasn't assigned to their groups or activities, but had the opportunity to watch from across the auditorium or gymnasium as they interacted with peers. By being involved, I also earned the right to talk to their counselors and leaders. Because of my time as a volunteer, I learned stuff about my kids I might have never otherwise known.

Two other great benefits are worth mentioning. One, you get to know your kids' friends. That brings great peace of mind...or alerts you to possible bad influences. Two, being part of that world gives you stuff to talk about that is *just yours*. Mom and siblings are out of the loop. You can certainly clue your wife in on what's going on, but keep some things just between you and your weekly carpool partner.

Also, you may discover a personal ministry that extends beyond your role as a father. Not too many years from now, your children will be up and out of the house. God may call you back to serve in those same hallways, gyms, lunchrooms, and auditoriums. There's a high probability that you'll make a difference in the lives of children who need some love and wisdom from a dad just like you.

Finally, don't be surprised if a few more years down the road you find yourself volunteering to be a monitor, mentor, or games leader for a new generation of kids—including your own grandchildren.

Say or Write "Love You"

*A word fitly spoken is like apples of gold
in settings of silver.*
PROVERBS 25:11 NKJV

I n her 2006 book *The Female Brain*, researcher and professor Louann Brizendine claims that on average, women speak 20,000 words a day compared with 7,000 for men. In 2010, the Pew Research Center found that teenage girls typically send and receive 80 texts per day, compared with 30 for teenage boys. Women are also much more likely to handwrite a letter or thank-you note. All of which means a few words from Dad are worth their weight in gold.

So, Dad, take that hint and start delivering short, encouraging phrases to your kids on a regular basis. I know you already say, "Have a great day" as they head out the door. You may even say, "Sweet dreams" or "Sleep tight" at the end of the day. But maybe it's time to mix it up a bit and add a few more expressions to your spoken-word repertoire. In the next few days, try a few of these fathering phrases out on your kids.

"You make me smile."

"I am so proud of you."

"Where did you learn to do that? That's fantastic."

"I look around and can't believe how lucky I am to be part of this family."

"You did that? That's epic!"

"Well played."

"You probably don't even realize how much your little brother looks up to you."

"Hey, sweetheart, come over here and tell me about your day."

"Hey, champ, come over here and tell me about your day."

"You are just about the best thing that ever happened to me!"

"That's a great idea. I wish I'd thought of it."

"I was thinking about you all day today."

"How did that geography quiz go?"

"I'm glad I'm your dad."

"Praying for you."

"Good luck at tryouts."

"Thanks for being you."

"You are a gift from God."

"You're amazing."

"Love you."

It's okay to use the same endearing phrase 5,000 days in a row. Or come up with something new every day.

Sentiments of love, appreciation, and encouragement can be said right out loud as your kids head out into the world. Or you can whisper them as you tuck them in at night. Maybe even better, jot them on a yellow Post-it note and stick it on their mirror, desktop, lunch box, book bag, or steering wheel. Sticky notes are especially appreciated when busy dads and busy kids have schedules that never seem to match up.

Don't be surprised if they keep those sticky notes right where they are or collect them in a special place so they can feel your thoughtful message over and over for weeks to come.

Dad, I hope you know your good words can make a good day better and turn a bad day totally around.

Apologize When You Mess Up

*Make allowance for each other's faults, and forgive anyone
who offends you. Remember, the Lord forgave you, so
you must forgive others. Above all, clothe yourselves with
love, which binds us all together in perfect harmony.*
COLOSSIANS 3:13-14 NLT

Dads need to be good at apologizing. That's because we mess up more often than kids and moms put together.

Kids are still figuring life out, so really we can't fault them too much when they make mistakes. Trial and error is an important skill for kids. That's how they learn. As James Joyce said, "A man's errors are his portals of discovery." So let's all try to cut our kids slack when they fall short.

Most moms, of course, are not the risk takers dads are. Men of action—like you and me—forge ahead and speak our minds even when we haven't thought about all the possible consequences. Which leads to an occasional opportunity to model the art of the apology to our children.

So, Dad, when you mess up—and you will—apologize with sincerity. You'll be modeling an essential character trait. You'll be bringing peace back to your household. You'll be giving your bride and your kids an opportunity to extend grace. Which provides a bonus teachable moment regarding the grace of God.

Humbly thank your family for their kind and forgiving heart. Then point out how that reflects the character of God in their lives. He is also in the business of granting unmerited forgiveness. It's never a bad day when we acknowledge our need to be rescued from our sinful condition.

Isn't grace awesome?

Keep Promises

*Honor your father and mother. Then you will live a long,
full life in the land the LORD your God is giving you.*

EXODUS 20:12 NLT

I give my dad credit. He had a clever stalling tactic that guaranteed he never broke a promise. Time after time, whenever we kids asked him if we could do something or go somewhere, he would say, "We'll see." That noncommittal response is, well, noncommittal. My brother, my sisters, or I would walk away with an answer to our question that wasn't an answer at all.

Now, that may sound like a brilliant fathering strategy. It actually worked when we were smaller. But before long my siblings and I caught on and figured out he was really just saying no.

As a dad, I pledged never to say, "We'll see." Which meant I would often say, "Sure, we can do that." Unfortunately, sometimes we didn't. Which meant sometimes I broke my promise. If I didn't realize it, my kids would let me know. That's not a good feeling. And that's not what great dads do.

Well, after about four or five broken promises, I learned to make promises only when I could and would keep them. I haven't broken one since.

So I guess that's one more lesson my father taught me. The value of keeping promises. Thanks, Dad. I miss you.

By the way, the fifth commandment is the only commandment that comes with a promise. Share it with your kids. Some nonbiblical scholars interpret that verse, "Be excellent to your folks and get real estate."

Follow the Crowd

Keep my commands and you will live;
guard my teachings as the apple of your eye.
PROVERBS 7:2

The explorer in you wants to forge your own path. But sometimes the easy decision and best choice is to follow the crowds. All you have to do is be aware of that one annual event in your part of the world that every family does.

You don't have to remember it. The media will remind you. It won't be too expensive, and it's probably a simple day trip you can do on a weekend.

What events come to mind? In the Midwest, it's apple picking. On the Oregon Coast, it might be clam digging in the fall. May is National Strawberry Month. If you live near our nation's capital, early April ushers in the National Cherry Blossom Festival. The Indy 500 is Memorial Day weekend. At Augusta National in Georgia, the Masters is always booked for the weekend ending with the third Sunday in June.

Bird-watching families can check out the swallows returning to San Juan Capistrano on or about March 19 and the buzzards returning to Hinckley Ridge, Ohio, every March 15.

The Iditarod sets out from Anchorage in early March. The UFO Festival in Roswell, New Mexico, is in early July. Scattered across the country are hot-air balloon races, storytelling festivals, and Renaissance faires.

With a little research, a great dad can find annual events within a few hours' drive that will expose your kids to art, music, books, film, or dance. Or maybe your annual family tradition is to spend a day at your own county or state fair. That's actually a pretty sweet choice. Cotton candy and elephant ears for everyone!

Make Time for Them When They're Young. They'll Make Time for You Later.

*Give, and it will be given to you. Good measure, pressed down,
shaken together, running over, will be put into your lap. For
with the measure you use it will be measured back to you.*

LUKE 6:38 ESV

Opportunities to spend time with teenagers and young adults can be rare and precious. With a little foresight, Dad, you can establish a foundation for those interactions years before.

That point was driven home to me during the 14 years I had the privilege of producing a weekly radio broadcast with author, speaker, and apologist Josh McDowell.

During one of our recording sessions, Josh recalled a memory from decades earlier delivering a lesson that has stayed with me and made me a better dad. Maybe it will do the same for you.

The revelation came when Josh was a young father and the head of a growing new ministry. One afternoon, he was working on a book deadline, and his young son came into his office. Sean asked innocently, "Want to play, Dad?"

Like so many dads, Josh responded, "Son, Daddy's busy. How about a little later?"

Young Sean trotted off without complaining, and Josh returned to his manuscript. A minute or two later, Josh's wife, Dottie, came in, sat down, and shared some memorable words of wisdom. "Honey, Sean just told me you were too busy to play with him. I know this book is important, but I'd like to point something out."

"What's that?" Josh remembers saying with a bit of impatience because now his wife was keeping him from his all-important project.

Dottie continued, "Honey, you're always busy. You're a five-ring circus. You will always have a deadline to meet, a chapter to finish, a talk to prepare, and a trip somewhere. But, honey, you won't always have a two-year-old son who wants to sit in his daddy's lap and show you his new ball." Having made her point, she started to walk out, but then she stopped, turned, and left her startled husband with words that cut into his heart and stayed with him ever since. "You know, if you spend time with your kids now, they'll spend time with you later."

Not immediately, but about three minutes later, Josh found himself kneeling on the carpet next to his desk. He made a pledge before God that he has kept ever since. He told our production team and the radio audience, "Until that moment, I had often made a shortsighted vow to always put my family before my ministry. But that wasn't right. That wasn't God's plan for fathers. On my knees I said, 'God, I never ever again will put my family before my ministry.' In that moment of brokenness, God made it very clear that Kelly, Sean, Katie, Heather, and Dottie do not come *before* my ministry. They *are* my first ministry."

47

Carry Recent Photos
on Your Smartphone

He will turn the hearts of the parents to their children, and
the hearts of the children to their parents; or else I will
come and strike the land with total destruction.
MALACHI 4:6

Most guys have half a billion unorganized photos on their phone. If you're like me, yours include photos of grocery lists, model numbers off broken appliances, under-the-sink plumbing projects, prescription bottles, the label of my wife's preferred brand of cold medicine, wall plaques with clever witticisms, hailstones the size of quarters that landed on my front lawn, and yes, a few pics of animals and people.

Most of those photos were for my own personal reference. Some were intended to show to others. To inform. To brag. To identify.

For years, the only photo-sharing option was pulling out my wallet and showing those two-by-three-inch photos taken every year at my kids' schools. Those scary-looking photos were kept in my back pocket in my billfold behind murky translucent plastic.

Not too long ago, I finally ditched the wallet photos because my iPhone was much more convenient. Sort of. With my wallet, I knew where the photos were. With my iPhone, I had to swipe through row after row of images and maybe get lucky finding a photo that was not too embarrassing and less than two years old.

That's when I came up with the best idea in this book. Dad, on your smartphone, create an album called "For Show." Keep fewer than a dozen photos in it. Select clear, current pics that show your family with their best face forward. Literally. Because everyone knows how to swipe through photos, you can open that folder anytime and hand your phone to a new friend, colleague, or airplane seatmate. Go ahead and say, "Here's my family. Go ahead and swipe through. It's just ten photos." This concept is so user-friendly, it doesn't even feel like bragging.

When a dad carries photos of his family, three things happen.

One, you think about your children more. Every time you look at your phone, you're holding a piece of your family, a piece of your heart.

Two, your kids feel the connection. They know what's on your phone. They groan because they hate the way they look in that picture, but they're glad you're carrying it.

Three, it's a hedge of protection for your marriage. By showing pics of your family, you are telling the world you place a high value on your relationship with your wife and kids. You're off-limits to flirting. You're working to support a cause greater than yourself. You're more likely to head straight home after work. On road trips, you're more likely to go souvenir shopping and catch an earlier flight home than go to the strip clubs or barhop all night long. Your expense account might even reflect your more sensible lifestyle. It shouldn't be a surprise that management prefers to give promotions and increased responsibility to guys like that.

Dad, take your kids everywhere you go. Whether they're in a fat wallet or a slim iPhone, don't leave home without them.

Teach the Art of the Handshake

Peace I leave with you; my peace I give you. I do not give to you as the world gives. Do not let your hearts be troubled and do not be afraid.

JOHN 14:27

In the early part of your church service, are you given an opportunity to shake hands with the people around you? Some churches call it "passing the peace."

How do your kids do with that? It's actually a pretty good time to make sure they know how to shake hands and show respect to their elders. It's also a time when you can model all kinds of positive behavior. Non-silly handshakes. Eye contact. Inside voices. Polite smiles. Personal boundaries. How to meet new people. How to greet old friends. All in 20 seconds or less!

Of course, those things are modeled in the moment. But you teach them in private. Like so many father-to-child lessons, you don't want to embarrass your son or daughter by correcting or lecturing them in public. Your wisdom is rarely well received when delivered on a soapbox.

Kids learn best in a one-on-one conversation containing information they can apply in the near future. Say something like, "What do you think of shaking hands during the service?" Whatever their response, honor it and add to it.

Specifically, I would focus on eye contact, a firm grip, two hand pumps, and maybe a head nod. Let your kids know that at the "handshake of peace," all that needs to be spoken is one or two words, such as "Hi" or "Good morning."

Shaking hands is a life skill. If you don't teach it, Dad, who will?

Hold Tight/Hold Loose

A man can receive nothing unless it has been given him from heaven.
JOHN 3:27 NASB

Hey, Dad. I've got news for you. Your house, car, laptop, guitar, big-screen TV, leather jacket, credit cards, yacht, hammock, workbench, iPhone, baseball glove, and favorite coffee mug are not yours. Whether you believe in God or not, those things are on loan to you from him. So take good care of your stuff because someday you are going to be held accountable for how it was all used.

Knowing that you really don't own any of that stuff should help you hold it loosely. Be generous. Covet not. Don't waste your life gathering more and more worldly possessions and building bigger houses to hold it all. It can all be taken from you in an instant.

I've got more news for you. Your kids also are not yours.

Knowing that you really don't own your children should help you hold on to them loosely as well. And tightly. Grasp them close with everlasting hugs, endless hours of conversation, and permanent connections between your world and theirs. While simultaneously letting them go. Pray them over to God. Trust God so much that you stop forcing your plan onto your children's lives and surrender to his plan.

Heaven has given you great gifts. The best thing you can do is say thanks and then give those gifts right back.

50

Be Amazed When They Bring You a Bug, Dandelion, or Shiny Rock

[Jesus] said to them, "Let the little children come to me, and do not hinder them, for the kingdom of God belongs to such as these."
MARK 10:14

When was the last time you made an exciting new discovery? Well, your kids are learning something astonishing and new every day. A child's natural curiosity will continue for years until someone or something compels them to stop. Don't be that killjoy.

For sure, just about everything your little one encounters will be stuff you take for granted. But maybe it shouldn't be. Maybe we grown-ups should be more amazed every time we step outside. Maybe we shouldn't take rainbows, caterpillars, and pinecones for granted. All three represent God's promise for the future. Have you thought about that? Have you told your kids?

Dad, it's easy to get caught up in the busyness of life. Keeping the boss happy. Paying the bills. Volunteering. Maintaining friendships. Doing Bible study homework. Wondering why the furnace is clicking and the check engine light is flashing. Keeping your wife happy. I get it.

Years ago, I remember kneeling on my driveway, failing in my attempt to tighten a bolt on my lawnmower, and finally realizing I needed a metric wrench and not the standard SAE wrench in my hand. I had already made several trips to my basement workshop and was not happy. But that's when one of my boys brought me a creepy crawly he had found under a rock in the side yard. It was actually quite wondrous. And thankfully, I set aside my lawnmower maintenance frustration and shared in my son's wonder. Joining him in that moment may have taken all of two minutes. Best of all, instead of adding to my annoyance, it actually defused some of the ire.

Dad, if you minimize, mock, or ignore their silly and not-so-impressive discoveries, they will probably stop making them. And that would be a terrible shame.

Instead, be intentional about getting down on their level. See the world through their eyes. Join their backyard expeditions and attic explorations. Do it for them. Do it for yourself. Reacquaint yourself with some of that childlike wonder and creativity. Those are powerful forces, especially for adults. After studying a cocoon, dandelion puff-ball, or wasp nest over the weekend, don't be surprised if Monday on the job, your brain generates a creative solution to a major problem that has been vexing your entire department for months.

Applaud your son or daughter's inquisitiveness. Never dismiss their curiosity. Join them in their discoveries. If you let it happen, your children will help you see the world in a brand-new way. Through their eyes you just might make some new discoveries about your kids and about yourself. And gain a new appreciation for God's creation.

51

Schedule an Adventure

Declare his glory among the nations,
his marvelous deeds among all peoples.
1 CHRONICLES 16:24

Grade-school kids love hanging out with dad. Middle-school kids too. But by high school, dads can feel marginalized in the life of their teenager. Jam-packed schedules and long-range plans often do not include you, Dad. That shouldn't really be a surprise, and that season of disconnection and distance isn't a reason for panic or overreaction. On the other hand, this might be the time for some bold and dauntless action.

What might that be? How about a trip for two fulfilling a dream. Just Dad and teen. Make a three-day whitewater rafting trip through the Grand Canyon. Score some hard-to-get tickets to see a major sporting event: the Final Four, World Series, Super Bowl, Masters, or Indy 500. Take a long weekend in Manhattan or some other major metropolis for shows, shopping, museums, and urban exploration.

Consider your teen's passions or career goals. Together, plan a trip to Wyoming for an archaeological dig, the Florida Keys to study marine life, Cupertino to tour Apple Park, Israel to walk where Jesus walked, or wherever your son's or daughter's imagination suggests.

Perhaps the best idea is to do a weeklong mission trip. Appalachia. Haiti. Mexico. Sierra Leone. Russia. Wherever God is working. There's a good chance your church or another church in your area is planning a trip in the very near future.

Finally, plan this adventure *with* your teenager. Make the offer a pleasant surprise. But if you pull out plane tickets or book time off work without checking their schedule, you might find those dates are in conflict with other plans your teen may have, such as team tryouts, a special event, entrance exams, college testing, or something they've been looking forward to for quite a while. On the other hand, taking them out of school for a valuable learning experience with you is not out of the question.

Also, you don't want to invest this kind of time, energy, and money unless it's something they really want to do.

When it comes to money, you'd be surprised at how teenagers understand what's going on with family finances. Even if you say, "We'll do anything you want!" they'll find something that doesn't drain your savings. You may even have to insist they don't worry about the money and think big.

Bring it up. See what they say. Present it as a way to do something awesome, not as a plan to help you reconnect with them.

Last thought. Adventures and mission experiences with the entire family are worth the effort. But a dad spending a week traveling or working side by side with a coming-of-age son or daughter will lead to experiences and memories that will keep you on the same page and communicating openly for decades to come.

Try this with your oldest child. And don't be surprised if younger siblings start to count down the months until they get to do their own adventure with Dad.

Oh yeah…adventures with your bride need to be scheduled on occasion as well.

Make Your Home a Hangout

Let the little children come to me.
LUKE 18:16

Put a Ping-Pong table in the basement. Get ESPN. Get the latest Xbox or PlayStation version of Rock Band or some other karaoke game. Build a fire pit in your backyard and keep a stash of Hershey bars, graham crackers, and marshmallows. Maintain a rec room that's not filled with stuff that is breakable, stainable, or irreplaceable. When a crew of hungry teenagers comes over to hang out after a game, plan for homecoming, or do a group project, volunteer to spring for pizza. Stockpile junk food. I know one dad who fills a special freezer with five-gallon containers of ice cream.

What's the purpose of all this? You want to know your kids' friends. You want their friends to know you. You want *your* world to intersect with *their* world.

The goal is to establish a comfort zone in your home so kids have just enough privacy to feel like they can talk, laugh, share secrets, and make lifelong connections. Still, you need to be able to enter or pass through that space without too much of an apology. If you have a bag of Dilly Bars or a bowl of popcorn, that makes it even easier.

Finally, don't feel bad if your teenager has friends over to play a game or watch a movie and you're not invited. The kids are at your house, and that's a good thing!

Celebrate Rules

Athletes cannot win the prize unless they follow the rules.
2 TIMOTHY 2:5 NLT

Ask a bunch of seven-year-olds what they think of rules, and you'll get the expected response. Rules are no fun. Rules get in the way. Rules tell you things you can't do.

But as they get older—if they have parents, teachers, and coaches who love them—those same kids will discover that rules create crucial and helpful boundaries, organization, and foundations.

Rules can be based on scientific principles and save lives. "Don't mix bleach with ammonia" is a nice rule to know when you're cleaning. Chloramine vapor can literally kill you.

Rules can be prompted by human nature and protect resources. "Don't leave your bicycle in the driveway" prevents your bike from being stolen or getting rusty or crunched by your older brother trying to get home before curfew.

Rules can be established by experience and make for fair play. The infield fly rule was written after clever infielders began to intentionally drop pop fly balls in order to turn an easy double play.

Rules can contradict natural instinct and promote peaceful coexistence. "Don't throw sand" increases the chances that a child won't go friendless at the sandbox or beach.

Our kids should expect, learn, applaud, and take advantage of rules.

Learn the rules of science, and you make new discoveries. Learn the proper technique for glassblowing, throwing pots, or welding, and you can sculpt evocative pieces of art. Learn how chess pieces move, and you can advance beyond checkers. Learn how to throw a knuckle curve, slider, and changeup, and the scouts will show up at your high-school diamond.

Without rules, chaos reigns. Without rules, every inventor, artist, scholar, or athlete would have to start from square one. There would be no record of past achievement. Without rules, you wouldn't know whether you had done something that had never been done before. Without rules, we couldn't keep score. (And then how would we know who won the homecoming football game last Friday night?)

In his second letter to Timothy, Paul makes an excellent case for following rules: "Athletes cannot win the prize unless they follow the rules" (2 Timothy 2:5 NLT).

So, let's all agree that rules are good things. As a great dad, you'll want to make sure your kids know that some choices are right and some choices are wrong. There is a reason for rules.

Still, Dad, as they get older, you should expect your children to go through one last season of testing the rules before they claim adulthood. It may be a few days in middle school. It may be a summer hanging out with the wrong crowd in high school. It may be a wasted semester in college. It may be the entire decade of their twenties. Your children will surely spend a season of life wrestling with rules. See if you can be close by to catch them before they land too hard and break themselves into a million pieces.

54

Teach Appropriate Rule Breaking

Remind the people to be subject to rulers and authorities,
to be obedient, to be ready to do whatever is good.

TITUS 3:1

Adults see warning labels, point-by-point instructions, and posted restrictions as good things, right? These things help make sure fewer kids fall out of roller coasters, salmonella won't spoil your picnic, and pizzas are golden brown on the bottom and properly melted on top. No one really enjoys assembly instructions from IKEA, but we fully realize that step-by-step is sometimes the best approach.

Young people, on the other hand, often have a distrust for rules. They want to explore new vistas and soar to new heights. That's one of the great joys of youth. When kids dream new dreams, they are just doing their job. We shouldn't throw cold water on their imagination. Kids don't want to hear that it's a bad idea to make toaster waffles in the bathtub or jump off the garage roof with a bedsheet parachute. Kids think rules stifle creativity and ingenuity.

As a dad, you want your kids to be safe, but you also want them to explore the world fearlessly. You want them not to be bogged down by conventional wisdom and oppressive regulations, but to chase extravagant dreams. You know that sometimes rules are meant to be broken.

So how do you reconcile those two opposites? Somehow explain to your kids that the first step in appropriately *breaking* rules is to *learn* the rules.

Henry Ford had to fully understand the way cars were built before he invented the assembly line. The Wright brothers had to know the physics of gravity before they conquered it. Great jazz musicians need to master their instrument before they take off on a wild, unrehearsed riff. Before Douglas Engelbart invented the computer mouse, he had to know the intricacies of computer interface technology.

Put another way, you can't make a better mousetrap until you really consider the whys and hows of a classic mousetrap.

This idea could lead to an eye-opening conversation with your curious, creative teenager. Start by saying, "Hey, Molly, my radical rule-breaking daughter, I have some thoughts to share." She will look at you skeptically. But then continue your little speech. "No, really. These are thoughts you'll want to hear. I'm about to give you permission to do whatever you want, whenever you want." And then walk her through the value of both keeping and breaking rules.

The punchline of your conversation is that your son or daughter needs to stay in school, keep practicing, continue to seek knowledge, and even pursue biblical wisdom to know right from wrong. Then they'll have all the information they need to break the rules at the right time and the right place.

Or as my editor might put it, "Jay, you need to *know* the rules of grammar before you *break* the rules of grammar." And that's why he sometimes allows me to begin a sentence with a conjunction, to occasionally split an infinitive, and once in a while to use a preposition to end a sentence with. See what I did there?

55

Be a Warrior

*Children born to a young man are like arrows in a warrior's hands.
How joyful is the man whose quiver is full of them! He will not be
put to shame when he confronts his accusers at the city gates.*

PSALM 127:4-5 NLT

You probably know that the long pouch on the back of an archer that holds his arrows is called a quiver. If you have a full quiver—lots of kids—you have a great shot at a life filled with joy. And if you started having babies as a young man, you have an even better shot at being a warrior archer. What's more, just the fact that you have a hefty amount of children means that down by the city gates (or barbershop or favorite beverage purveyor) you will win most arguments against those who might confront you.

The bow-wielding warrior is a great image for fathers to emulate. Look again at Psalm 127:4-5. Let's meditate on those words for a moment.

You're an archer. You are young, strong, and confident. You reach over your shoulder and extract a single arrow from your quiver. You crafted that arrow with care and loaded that quiver yourself, so you know the shaft is straight and true, the feathered fletching precise. Still, you slide your fingers down the narrow cylinder in preparation for a flawless flight. You've spent many hours disciplining yourself, so it feels natural to slide the notch of the arrow onto the bowstring. Combining strength and gentleness, you pull that arrow toward you, close to your heart. With great care you choose a target that's exactly right for this arrow. You remain steadfast, feet planted firm. With a slight smile, you let the beloved arrow fly. Your assignment as a warrior complete.

That was so much fun. You do it again. And again…with each one of your kids. Until your quiver is empty, just as God planned.

Now, mighty warrior, here's the question. Which of those archery activities is your strength, and which might be your weakness? Teaching truth to your kids? Disciplining yourself and standing on solid ground? Opening your heart and pulling your kids toward you? Helping them each find the right target? Or letting them go to find their own way?

Each dad has his own strengths and weaknesses. That's why we need to work together, lift each other up, share our experiences and frustrations, and pray for guidance. Some men in your sphere of influence are desperate dads trying to raise sons and daughters to follow Christ. Don't be afraid to *ask* for help and *offer* help to a fellow warrior.

Yes, we're in a battle. But we don't have to go it alone.

Wake Your Kid for a Lunar Eclipse

Who has measured the waters in the hollow of his hand,
or with the breadth of his hand marked off the heavens?
Who has held the dust of the earth in a basket,
or weighed the mountains on the scales and the hills in a balance?

ISAIAH 40:12

Quiz. Let's say it's a school night and you hear the sky will be clear for a dramatic view of a rare lunar eclipse at two a.m. Does your child's mom want you to wake your second grader? Of course not. But should you? Absolutely. Children that age love making new discoveries and having the inside scoop on what happens after dark.

I encourage you, Dad, to shuffle them over to the window or drag them out on the front lawn so they can see for themselves what happens when the sun, earth, and moon line up. You don't have to watch the entire thing. But do make sure they see enough that they understand what's going on.

The next day at school, when the teacher wonders why your child falls asleep at their desk, your son or daughter will simply say, "My dad got me up for the lunar eclipse." The teacher will smile and shake her head. All the other kids will be jealous. And your child will remember that event forever.

By the way, as the two of you look up into that night sky, don't forget to mention who placed each star. Remind your precious child that you love them to the moon and back. And so does that Creator God.

See the Glory

For the Lord is the Spirit, and wherever the Spirit of the Lord is, there is freedom. So all of us who have had that veil removed can see and reflect the glory of the Lord. And the Lord—who is the Spirit—makes us more and more like him as we are changed into his glorious image.

2 CORINTHIANS 3:17-18 NLT

Are you a new dad, up to your knees in dirty diapers, baby bottles, and stained bibs, with a young wife mired in postpartum depression?

Are you the hardworking father of sprouting children, trying to build a career while also being a model parent—feigning interest at back-to-school night, scratching your head over math homework, dramatizing bedtime stories, and racing to the office-supply store before it closes for poster board and markers?

Are you the dad of a teenager, regularly tossing car keys across the kitchen, pacing the floor after missed curfews, opening your home to mobs of voracious adolescents, worrying about teen sex, and thinking about how you're ever going to pay for college?

New dad, one evening you're going to look across the room at your beautiful, exhausted wife rocking that baby and singing a sweet lullaby. In that moment, God will reveal to you the amazing gift of new life and family. That's glory.

Hardworking, busy dad, one evening you will look up to see one of your children and a friend playing Scrabble, another child noodling on the piano, your older child finishing up some algebra homework at the kitchen table, and your wife reading in her favorite chair. God will be telling you that everything you do is worth the effort. That's glory.

Dad of teenagers, one day soon you're going to have a reasonable, thoughtful adult conversation with your growing son or daughter. Their maturity, poise, and sound judgment will stun you. In that moment, God will invite you to trust in the future he has planned. That's glory.

Watch for it, Dad. Don't be overwhelmed. Instead, let those moments of realization send you to your knees in awe and gratitude. Surrender control of your family to God. Be broken before the Creator, who promises to rebuild you and empower you to be the great dad he is calling you to be.

Enjoy that new perspective as a fully devoted dad. Expect your family to provide you with undeserved moments of shared laughter, surprising generosity, newly discovered giftedness, sudden spiritual insights, wisdom beyond their years, and hugs for no reason at all.

That's glory. Don't miss it.

58

Sing Lullabies

*Sing a new song to the L*ORD*!*
Sing his praises from the ends of the earth!

ISAIAH 42:10 NLT

The following lyrics to five very short songs were never meant to be published in a book. I wrote these words during five highly emotional periods of my life. They were first sung in a whisper in a maternity ward. Except for the first one, these songs were all written on the days my kids were born. Alec's song was written two days after his birth as I rocked him in the neonatal intensive-care unit at Lutheran General Hospital. I remember it like it was yesterday.

> Alec, Alec, my little pal.
> Alec, Alec, I love you so.
> © 1980 Jay K. Payleitner

> Randy, Randy, you're my boy.
> Randy, Randy, my pride and joy.
> © 1983 Jay K. Payleitner

> Max, Max, it's a fact.
> You're my guy. You're my…Max!
> © 1986 Jay K. Payleitner

> Isaac, Isaac, God smiled.
> On my son, Isaac Jay.
> © 1988 Jay K. Payleitner

> Rae Anne, Rae Anne, ray of sunshine.
> My little girl, brightens each day.
> © 1993 Jay K. Payleitner

Dad, even if you can't carry a tune in a bucket, don't let Mom be the only one to sing lullabies to your babies. Your little ones—and maybe your teenagers—should know your singing voice. From lullabies to worship songs to the national anthem, music is a heartfelt way to connect with your kids and bring your family together.

Also, don't feel like you have to come up with a personal song for each of your kids. Just sing your favorite classic rock song, hymn, or TV theme song, as long as it's sung with a smile and gentle voice. But I must say, melodically whispering your newborn's name as you hold them close is a great way to start a life and a relationship.

To Alec, Randall, Max, Isaac, and Rae Anne: Sorry, the secret's out. Your song—written for your ears only—is now immortalized in this book that will be read by dads everywhere. But really, only the lyrics are public. The tune is still in my head. And yours.

59

Notice the Good Stuff
and Let Them Know

When I was a child, I spoke and thought and reasoned as a child. But when I grew up, I put away childish things. Now we see things imperfectly, like puzzling reflections in a mirror, but then we will see everything with perfect clarity. All that I know now is partial and incomplete, but then I will know everything completely, just as God now knows me completely.

1 CORINTHIANS 13:11-12 NLT

The Bible has all kinds of rules you can use to bash your kids over the head. "Do this. Don't do that. Act a certain way." The rules are valid and valuable. They're written for our instruction and theirs. But sometimes those rules can feel like a burden. Especially to kids like yours, who are doing pretty well and making pretty good choices.

Wouldn't it be nice to pull out the Bible and show our children a verse that makes them feel like they're headed in the right direction? Don't we all like to hear some positive reinforcement every once in a while?

Well, next time your son or daughter does something that reveals a new level of maturity, turn to 1 Corinthians 13:11-12 and share it. Read it together. Tell them you noticed. Let them know that not long ago, they were little. They're growing up. And you love seeing the way God is working in their lives.

That sneak peek at your growing child's new maturity could occur when they see something around the house that needs to get done and they do it themselves. Without any adult interaction. For example, mowing the lawn, cleaning the kitchen, picking up dog poop, changing a lightbulb, sorting recyclables, bringing in the trash cans from the curb, and so on. They saw a need, and they took care of it.

Evidence of a new maturity could be when they voluntarily take on a new challenge outside their comfort zone: organizing a food drive, volunteering in the church nursery, tithing ten percent of their baby-sitting money, taking a position of leadership in their youth group, or going out of their way to visit a grandparent, great-grandparent, or other older person.

When your child surprises you with grown-up behavior, don't be so surprised! But do take them quietly aside and say, "Hey, I noticed. And I'm glad to be your dad." Tell them you're looking forward to seeing how God will use them in the next several years.

Also, remind them there's no hurry to leave childhood behind, but it's a joy to see them growing in maturity and grace. If it's your style, you can even joke that they're growing up too fast and ask them to stay little.

Remind them also that even adults don't have all the answers. But as the above verse promises to all believers, someday "we will see everything with perfect clarity."

60

Foster Sportsmanship

*We can rejoice, too, when we run into problems and trials,
for we know that they help us develop endurance.*
ROMANS 5:3 NLT

Teaching your kids to be good sports when they win is easy, right? Well, maybe not. Being a good winner is certainly not automatic. Touchdown dances, trash talking, and chest thumping have gotten out of hand in professional sports, and young athletes love to emulate those multimillionaires. Which is why dads need to step in early and model respect for players on both teams and respect for the sport itself.

Here's one strategy for teaching good sportsmanship: Appreciate and point out excellence by any player on the field or court whether they're on your favorite team or the opposing team. Watching a game with your child, go ahead and cheer the spectacular plays. But also make note of players who hustle, lay down the perfect sacrifice bunt, use proper footwork, know when to stop the clock, and make their teammates look good.

If you get a chance to coach your children's teams, never allow one of your players to mock an opponent. Celebrating after a win is fair, but make sure the team handshakes are respectable.

I'm not denying that emotions can elevate during a well-played matchup. Win or lose, there's going to be leftover energy that needs to go somewhere. Whether you're a coach or spectator, do what you can to help young athletes channel those emotions.

For the winning team, it may be valuable to use that energy to make sure every member of the team feels like part of the celebration. That includes showing appreciation to coaches, team managers, statisticians, and so on.

Even before the season begins, team members should anticipate that losing is not all bad. A good coach will see a tough loss as a chance to build character and deliver fresh wisdom to his or her players.

Watch what happens after a close Little League or high school baseball game. The teams jog out to right field and left field and everyone takes a knee. The winning team has a short meeting with lots of high fives and very little instruction. The losing coach goes quite a bit longer, pointing out skills that need improvement and prioritizing which areas to work on during the next practice. You've seen it dozens of times.

There's a good chance that both teams made mental and physical errors during the game. But only members of the losing team *learned* something after the game. The winners didn't. The next day, the losing coach is going to push his team a little harder—the winning coach may not.

It's no fun to lose. But I daresay, if the losing coach is getting the job done, the next time those two teams play, the result is going to be different.

Worth noting, Dad: After a disappointing performance, the last thing you want to do is throw a bunch of clichés at your kid. But the fact is that while it's fun to win, most improvement happens because you don't want to lose again.

61

Connect Your Kids to Your Parents

One generation commends your works to another;
they tell of your mighty acts.

PSALM 145:4

I n many families, grandparents and grandkids connect naturally. Your parents or in-laws live nearby and are eager to engage the kids, and vice versa. My own mom and dad modeled this beautifully, and as a new gramps, I've experienced it firsthand in the past few years.

The benefits are many. Grandparents often have unique skills they can pass along. They are an extra set of eyes that may notice opportunities or concerns regarding your kids. Their memories help ground young people in your family heritage, especially through stories of survival and perseverance. Growing up, you may have turned up your nose at Mom and Dad's hobbies and interests, but grandkids may find those activities enchanting.

The archetype of a grandparent spoiling a grandchild is honorable. It really is okay for Grandma to say yes even though Mom would usually say no. Kids fully realize they're "getting away with murder," and they shouldn't expect the same luxuries at home.

If you have more than one kid, the time your son or daughter spends with grandparents becomes even more special. You may not always have time to listen, but Grandpa does.

Other benefits include free babysitting, a helping hand in an emergency, and an experienced sounding board about issues relating to home buying, education, finances, health, and other life decisions. In other words, Grandma might be able to tell the difference between chicken pox and scabies. (Still, you probably want to check with a doctor.)

Another great benefit is that watching how your parents love and care for your kids can give you a fresh appreciation for who they are, which might help heal some old battle scars from when you were a teenager or young adult.

Finally, you can expect your parents to share stories with your kids from when you were their age. That's actually a good thing. It's comforting for kids to imagine their mom or dad going through a certain amount of middle-school angst and teenage rebellion. They just might think, *Maybe my parents do understand.*

So how do you harvest all those benefits? Again, if you make the time, many of those connections will happen naturally. If distance or regrets from the past get in the way, you may have some extra work to do. Make those cross-country trips. Mend those fences. Skype. Call. Apologize for harsh words spoken years ago. Make the effort to connect the generations.

And, if your own grandparents are still around, take every opportunity to connect them with their great-grandchildren. Back at the old homestead or the retirement center, ask open-ended questions that help uncover a few unspoken memories. Too often those times together include way too much talk about the weather, today's news headlines, or their latest physical ailments. Kids don't want to hear that. Keep the conversation going until the family patriarch tells a story or two that even you have never heard before. Don't delay. Those memories fade when you least expect it.

Be Humble

A man's pride will bring him low,
but a humble spirit will obtain honor.
PROVERBS 29:23 NASB

There will come a turning point in your child's life that you may not immediately perceive. It's that moment when they move from "Dad knows everything" to "Dad doesn't know what he's talking about." Not coincidentally, that comes right around the middle-school years.

Don't panic, Dad. Yes, it's fun being the guy who has all the answers. But it can be even more fulfilling to be the guy your son or daughter comes to when seeking a partner in finding answers and making new discoveries. Suddenly you're working side by side, seeking solutions to issues complex or not so complex. You're saying things like "What do you think?" and "For years, I used to do it this way, but I'm not sure that works anymore."

When you set your pride aside and ask your child's opinion, you're giving them a tremendous gift. You're empowering them. You're modeling curiosity and teamwork. You're equipping them to be lifelong learners. You're setting them up for success.

Maybe most importantly, you're increasing the chances they will come to you for advice and guidance somewhere down the road of life. You know...when things really matter.

So don't mourn the passing of the know-it-all dad. And make sure he stays far, far away. If your son or daughter invites him back for a short visit, that's good news. But stay humble, Dad. A humble dad is worthy of trust, respect, and honor.

Read a Well-Worn Bible

*All Scripture is God-breathed and is useful for teaching, rebuking,
correcting and training in righteousness, so that the servant
of God may be thoroughly equipped for every good work.*

2 TIMOTHY 3:16-17

G rab your personal study Bible—if you can find it—and assess its physical appearance.

Might I suggest the condition of your personal faith journey is inversely proportional to the condition of your Bible. In other words, the more wear and tear, the better.

Certainly, you need to respect the book itself. But you should feel comfortable cracking it open, underlining passages, and writing notes in the margin. Hebrews 4:12 says, "The word of God is living and active" (NASB). But if your Bible stays trapped in the dark corner of a bookshelf, it has not had the chance to bring light into your life.

Please don't judge your neighbor on the condition of his Bible. His online Bible may get lots of hits. He may be on a brand-new edition, having worn out five others in his lifetime. Or he may be a new Christian, about to embark on the extraordinary adventure of digging into God's Word for the first time.

An even bigger point to remember is this: Just *reading* the Bible doesn't cut it. What we read needs to impact how we think and what we do. "Do not merely listen to the word, and so deceive yourselves. Do what it says" (James 1:22).

Still, there's nothing like a well-worn, well-read, well-loved Bible.

You know those comfy jeans you love so much? Your Bible should feel just that comfortable. Even when its challenges make you uncomfortable.

64

Cherish Chauffeur Chatting

Fools find no pleasure in understanding
but delight in airing their own opinions.
PROVERBS 18:2

Some of the best conversations I've had with my kids took place when they were riding shotgun while we ran errands or drove to a school function, church event, or sports practice.

Today that's impossible with younger kids because of government-mandated child restraint laws. Every state is different, but some require kids as old as 12 to sit in the backseat. I'm not challenging these laws. Of course, we all want children to be safe. But you can't have a casual conversation about hopes, dreams, fears, and frustrations with a kid who's four feet behind you in a noisy car.

Which means there's cause for celebration when your child graduates from the backseat to the front. That celebration should also include a new set of rules...or at least a conversation that sets some explicit expectations. Specifically, you'll want some rules when it comes to that multifunctional smartphone to which all kids are attached these days.

As an aside: Each family has to determine *when* it's the right time for kids to get their own phone. And it may not be the same time for every kid. It's about responsibility, maturity, extracurricular activities, and safety. Whether they whine real loud or all their friends have phones should not impact your decision.

When it comes to phone use in the car, the goal is to minimize your child's texting, gaming, tweeting, Instagramming, Googling, posting, and talking. Especially when it's just the two of you. But you can't just set limits without reason, and you'll want to come to some kind of agreement.

Be honest. Talk about how valuable time in the car is for both of you to catch up with each other—especially as your lives get busier. Don't deny the importance of communicating with their friends and team-mates. Get them to agree that phones can be a distraction. Make sure they acknowledge that you're paying the bills, you're the parent, and you have ultimate authority of that magic microcomputer and com-munication device they cherish so dearly. Maybe even joke that—as a driver—you can't be on the phone, so it's not fair they get to use theirs.

So what's the rule? It's actually pretty simple. If their phone rings or a text arrives, your son or daughter can respond as needed. That's com-mon courtesy. But outgoing texts or conversations can be initiated only after parental approval, which means your young traveling compan-ion would need to explain whom they are contacting and why. Also, of course, no gaming, posting, or engaging in favorite apps at any time during your excursions.

Here's what they need to recognize: Your kid in your car cannot ignore you, whip out their phone, and start typing, texting, scrolling, or gaming on a whim. It's just rude.

Because they are approaching adulthood, you can explain that there will likely be exceptions to these rules and you'll gladly talk them out. That's what adults do. It's called mutual respect.

Of course, there's always the option of confiscating their precious device for noncompliance. They know that, right?

65

Be a Little Ticked Off Sometimes

Then [Jesus] returned to the disciples and found them asleep. He
said to Peter, "Couldn't you watch with me even one hour?"
MATTHEW 26:40 NLT

This verse describes an amazing scene. Even more amazing if you consider what Jesus had already been through that night. At the Last Supper, he washed feet, broke bread, shared wine, confirmed his earthly mission, and pointed out the men who would betray and deny him.

Then he invited Peter, James, and John to accompany him to the Garden of Gethsemane. Jesus asked them to stay and keep watch, walked deeper into the Garden, fell on the ground to pray, asked God if the events about to unfold were really necessary, and sweat blood.

All he wanted was for a few of his chosen disciples to say awake for 60 minutes. They didn't do it. And Jesus let them know in no uncertain terms that he was disappointed.

Now there's a lot more to it than that, but let's just see if there's a lesson for fathers in there someplace.

It's okay to let our kids know when they have let us down. Let me say that again because our society suggests we shouldn't make our kids feel bad.

It's okay to let our kids know when they have let us down.

Of course, we don't want to pile on our kids every time they make a mistake. And they should never question our unconditional love. But there are proactive steps we can take to turn a negative situation positive.

Be clear about what they did wrong. Assert your authority. If there's any doubt, point out the damage that may have occurred: hurt feelings, lost trust, property damage, and so on. Let them know whether there will be repercussions. Make sure the punishment fits the crime. Give them a chance to make it right. Urge them to apologize. If they do, forgive them.

In the process, your son or daughter may come up with all kinds of excuses or reasons why it's not their fault. Kids are good at that. In most cases, you should listen and help them understand how better decisions might have kept the situation from going from bad to worse. If they are frequent excuse makers, let them know they are not doing themselves any favors.

The key is to focus on their actions. We never want to label our kids as failures. But if we have set clear expectations and clear deadlines, and we've caught them in the act of dropping the ball, then we have the right—and even the responsibility—to let them know. We need to be able to say, "Colin, I asked you to do this. What's going on?" Or "Abby, this should have been done by now. I need you to make it right."

Sometimes it's not easy being a dad. You need to figure out a way to confront your children in love, firmness, and grace.

66

Applaud Artistic Beauty

God created mankind in his own image, in
the image of God he created them.
GENESIS 1:27

Has one of your children demonstrated a flair for art—especially painting, sculpting, fiction writing, or performance? Congratulations! There are so many beautiful opportunities for your child to celebrate life, love, imagination, and God's creation. But sometimes that's not the choice they make.

With grade-school kids, there's rarely a problem. They like rainbows, trees, birds, fishes, and smiles. But sometime during their early teens, many growing artists discover they can grab some extra attention with very little effort. A blood-spattered painting. A poem about suicide. Lyrics with words they would never speak but will readily sing. Dad, don't panic. Just realize they're flexing their creative muscles and testing boundaries. How you respond is important. I recommend you respond as a curious fan. Ask questions. Clarify what they're trying to say. In some cases, it actually might be a cry for help. But most of the time, it's a test. They're testing the power of their art. And they're testing the authority figures in their life.

In public, be an observer. In private, take a stand. Acknowledge the power of their work. Let them know they are responsible for what they create. Help them understand the difference between creating something of lasting beauty and the degradation of shock art. If it helps and if they can handle it, talk with your young artist about examples of so-called art that lack any true value. Slasher movies, torture porn novels, and hip-hop lyrics that demean women are all examples of "creativity" that's really not very creative.

Every painting doesn't have to be filled with daisies. Every movie doesn't have to end with the hero and heroine riding off into the sunset. Choreography should sometimes leave the dancer off-balance. A symphony should include some dissonance. Art should investigate and comment on the struggles of life. But if your son or daughter identifies as an artist, they have a responsibility to leave their audience glad they were witness to that art. If the person who experiences any kind of art feels like they need to take a shower after attending an exhibit, watching a video, or hearing a song, the artist has failed.

The human ability to create exists only because we were made in the image of the Creator. Dad, you are in a unique position to help your kids uncover their creative gifts…and harvest them to build God's kingdom and give glory back to him.

The answer is not to censor our kids, but to help them see the power they have. Beyond just protecting them from the dark forces that would subvert art, let's equip them to battle against those forces.

Which means first helping our children open their hearts and minds to things worthy of praise. Then helping them discover the beauty of God's creation—including themselves. Which will give them confidence to create new, uplifting art using their own gifts and passions. Then suddenly, because of your children, some of the dark corners of the world will have a few less shadows.

67

Knock and Pray

Truly I tell you that if two of you on earth agree about anything
they ask for, it will be done for them by my Father in heaven. For
where two or three gather in my name, there am I with them.
MATTHEW 18:19-20

Sometime soon, knock on your son or daughter's bedroom door and say something like, "I need a quiet place to pray. Can I hang out here for about two minutes?" They may look up slightly confused, but their response will probably be, "Umm...I guess so."

Then do it. Walk in, sit on the edge of their bed, and almost as if they're not there, start praying, using actual words. Pray for your situation at work, your wife, your other kids, your own stresses, a neighbor, and anything else. End with a prayer for your child who is sitting right there with you. Thank them, kiss their forehead, and leave quietly and gracefully.

Does that sound impossible? Allow me to give you an example of how that might work.

> Heavenly Father, thank you for the generosity and love you keep pouring on our family. I'm humbled and grateful. I'm challenged to serve you as best I can.
>
> You know how the site management project at work is stressing me out. Lord, I ask for patience and new direction there.
>
> For my family, Lord, you know Tim is waiting to hear back about those college applications. Help him trust you and make the right choice for next fall. And for Tammy, help me be the husband she needs. What a gift she is to me and our kids. Please God, continue to bless our marriage.

For Mr. Bradley's surgery, for safe travels next week as I head to Pittsburgh, for the election next month…Lord, please let your will be done.

Finally, for Emily. You've given her such a tender heart for others and a great sense of humor. Help her just have a great weekend.

Thank you, Lord, for loving us so much and including us in your family. Thank you for preparing a place for all of us to be united with you for eternity in heaven. I pray this in the name of your Son, Jesus. Amen.

Now, that wasn't so hard, was it? Your child may have been stunned by the experience. Or maybe it made perfect sense. In any case, that two minutes achieves several worthy goals. You prayed. You modeled how to pray. You entered their world. You allowed them to enter your world. You let them know your marriage is strong. You reminded them that other members of the family have concerns equal to or greater than theirs. You let them know your schedule. And you presented heaven as a place where love is alive and families are reunited. Plus, prayers like that just might help unleash supernatural forces—such as legions of guardian angels—within the walls of that bedroom.

Perhaps best of all, you have earned the right to return in the near future to knock and pray again.

68

Rescue Them at the Top
of Any Slippery Slope

*Those who won't care for their relatives, especially
those in their own household, have denied the true
faith. Such people are worse than unbelievers.*

1 TIMOTHY 5:8 NLT

Dads should never stick their head in the sand. We need to notice when our kids have messed up. Often, we even need to anticipate when they're *about* to mess up.

Sometimes that means stepping in and preventing a disaster. Sometimes that means letting your kids make mistakes and learn from them. After all, most of us learned our greatest lessons by making mistakes and surviving them.

By the way, Dad, you won't be able to anticipate every bad decision your kids are going to make. So please don't beat yourself up when your kid does something boneheaded or worse. You raised them right, so by the time you get wind of their poor choice, they may have already taken steps to apologize, mitigate damages, and make the necessary changes so it doesn't happen again.

Still, one of the great dad challenges of all time is to walk the tightrope of too much or too little vigilant parenting. You want to nip negative behavior early, rescuing them at the top of any slippery slope. On the other hand, you want to equip them to self-police and make wise decisions on their own. After all, you're not always going to be there to stop them from taking a dare, walking into that tattoo parlor, posting an inappropriate photo, investing in swampland, or talking back to the traffic cop.

Here's a guiding principle that has served me well: A father needs to intervene if the aftermath is life-threatening, permanently damaging to their reputation and witness, or likely to cause them to miss a major opportunity in the near future. However, if their mess-up leads to some minor frustration with a coach, a failed grade on a homework assignment, or a friend with hurt feelings, then let them work it out for themselves. You can suggest they talk it out with the coach, teacher, or friend. But don't make any phone calls or rush to rescue your son or daughter. Especially if they don't ask for your help.

It's usually advantageous to let natural consequences take their course. That lets you off the hook. With natural consequences, you don't have to be the bad guy or come up with just the right punishment. Once the lesson is learned, you always have the option to step in and offer a word of encouragement or a helping hand. If they seem to have gotten away with poor behavior, you may need to add further consequences.

All of this is one more reason to know your child. Understand that some slopes—things like drugs, alcohol, violent behavior, vandalism, sexual promiscuity, and gang involvement—are terrifyingly slippery. Know that your child is counting on you to be their hero. Whether they say it or not.

Remember the Carousel

Some trust in chariots and some in horses,
but we trust in the name of the LORD our God.

PSALM 20:7

The first few times your son or daughter rides a merry-go-round, you ride with them. You stand beside their painted pony, making sure the centrifugal force doesn't send them flying off into the guardrail.

And then one day, that little boy or girl wants to do the ride without you.

In one life-changing moment, they are no longer holding onto Dad's strong hand or Mom's secure apron strings. When the ride begins with a cacophony of garish colors and noise, you child is whooshed out of sight. They're gone. On their own.

But what happens on each revolution? As they come full circle, they look for you and loosen their grip with one hand just long enough to wave with delight.

How does a small child muster the courage to go it alone that first time? They have learned from experience that you are there in case they need to be rescued. Seeing you standing firm at every revolution provides the security they need and confirms the heart connection you need. The exuberant wave is not hello or goodbye—it's saying, "We're in this together."

So. Remember the carousel.

Embrace that image when your children do anything daring. Kindergarten. Their first sleepover. Summer camp. Their first date. Their first job. College. The mission field. The military. Be there to send them off and welcome them back.

Oh yeah…Dad, don't even think about *not* being there when the ride is over.

Kick Around Deep Ideas

The fear of the LORD is the beginning of knowledge.
PROVERBS 1:7

When was the last time you had a good old-fashioned philosophical discussion with your children? Even if your son or daughter is under seven, you can still get their brains working. Open-ended questions work well.

"What's the best way to learn how to do something?"

"What makes babies cry?"

"How would the world be different if animals could talk?"

"What's the most important holiday?"

"What color is love?"

Their responses might be puzzling, goofy, or deeply profound. Or maybe their little minds aren't yet ready to dig that deep. Still, just asking the question might trigger some new creativity or ingenuity. The goal is to start a discussion and help them see multiple sides of a question. In many cases, there are no right and wrong answers.

Beyond asking questions, you might want to present an occasional precept or truism. As kids get older, hit them up with these ideas:

"There's an entire apple orchard in every seed."

"If you hit the target every time, the target is too big."

"When trading baseball cards, the best deals are good for both sides."

"To experience light there must first be darkness."

"Don't let yesterday use up too much of today."

"Broken crayons still color."

"Be yourself because everyone else is already taken."

"A mousetrap always provides free cheese."

"If you chase two rabbits, both will escape."

Thought-provoking statements like these carry a simple truth and a deeper truth. See if your son or daughter can identify both.

When you run out of your own words of wisdom, you might want to turn to the great philosophers and theologians of centuries past. One of my favorite thoughtful precepts is from G.K. Chesterton's 1929 book *The Thing*. It is often summarized, "Don't take down a fence until you know why it was put up."

Presenting this idea to your kids, you might explain that Chesterton was a deep thinker from about 100 years ago. It was a time of great social change, and radical reformers wanted to throw out all the work done by the previous generations. They would look at an existing regulation or prohibition and discard it with little regard.

In response, Chesterton wisely made the case that before you move ahead with a new plan, it's a good idea to take a step back and look at the old plan. Try to determine its original purpose. *Then* make your decision.

In other words, maybe the old fence should be taken down. But maybe not. Said another way, maybe the existing methodology or laws are still vital and valid. Said still another way, change isn't always a good thing.

Of course, when you ask your children deep philosophical questions, you run the risk of receiving a barrage of groans and eye rolls in return. But just maybe you're igniting a fire in a corner of their brain. A fire that will burn bright when faced with future creative challenges or the need to defend the great truths of life.

At the very least, you're going to keep them guessing. And that's not a bad thing.

71

Invigorate Any Slugs

*Whatever you do, do your work heartily, as
for the Lord rather than for men.*
COLOSSIANS 3:23 NASB

There's a rumor going around that young people today are afraid of a little hard work. They don't want to get their hands dirty. They have an attitude of entitlement. They want something for nothing. But I'm not convinced.

Maybe we just think kids are lazy because the culture has changed since we were kids.

Growing up, our generation listened to our grandparents talk about the empty pantries of the Great Depression and the nationwide rationing of World War II. Our children can't imagine opening an empty cupboard or refrigerator.

In recent years, extracurricular activities have exploded, requiring long hours and seasons that never end, which means high-school kids don't have time for anything else.

Jobs around the house—lawn mowing, painting, housecleaning, even snow and leaf removal—are being hired out. Kids aren't expected to work, so they never learn how.

In an attempt to keep up with other families, parents buy whatever their kids need or want. The kids have no reason to save or get a job.

Technology keeps kids inside, making them only appear lazy.

All that to say, maybe your kids are not really slackers—they just haven't been convinced their contribution to the upkeep of the household will make a difference.

So what about your precious babies? Could they use a few calluses? How about a lesson in appreciating what they have?

If you're brave enough, plop down on the couch next to your chill-axing teen, open your Bible to Proverbs 13:4, and read, "The sluggard craves and gets nothing, but the desire of the diligent will be abundantly satisfied" (NET). Then politely ask, "Are you a slug, or do you just appear to be one?"

If they're still talking with you after that vicious attack on their lifestyle, then lay out some ground rules. Maybe call them "expectations."

As they get older, we should expect young people to be responsible for much of their own upkeep—their own laundry, getting themselves up and out the door, making their bed, cleaning up after themselves, and so on.

On top of that, don't forget to expect their eager participation in regular chores for the common good. That includes setting the table, washing dishes, taking out trash, mowing the lawn, sweeping the porch...whatever works for your family.

And, of course, expect them to jump to their feet anytime you announce a seasonal or one-time job to be completed. Things like hauling mulch, rototilling the garden, painting the fence, and scrubbing lawn furniture. All reasonable expectations for kids who take it for granted that your kitchen is well stocked with chips and soft drinks.

It all begins, of course, when they're about two years old and we expect them to pick up their cars, Legos, dinosaurs, puzzles, stuffed animals, and books, and put them away on shelves or in bins. Make it easy. Make it fun. Make it a routine. Make it an expectation.

72

Exemplify Glory and Rewards

Each generation tells of your faithfulness to the next.
ISAIAH 38:19 NLT

You've heard the statistics. When young people head off to college, the military, or their first career, way too many of them let their faith slide. Even if they were fairly active in church as a teenager, they turn their back on God. And parents feel like they've failed.

Without getting bogged down in numbers and percentages, there is a real sense that young adults today do not see any personal value in following the faith convictions of their moms and dads. They see little evidence that having a relationship with Jesus is worth the effort. The question worth asking is, why?

Dad, I think it might be our fault.

Too often, our outward appearance does not reflect our dependence on God. When good things happen, we love to take the credit. When bad things happen, we fix them. In private, we might reveal our brokenness and need for a Savior. Behind closed doors, we will pray, seek wise spiritual counsel, and surrender, even tearfully, to God's will. But in public—when we put on the persona seen by our kids—we rarely acknowledge our need for God.

As a result, our children do not see how he has been working in us, for us, and through us. Which means you can't blame them for not living under the glory, sanctification, and reward of being a follower of Christ.

Dad, have your children ever heard the story of how you hit bottom, acknowledged your broken condition, realized your need for redemption, felt genuine remorse, believed the truth of Scripture, and accepted Christ as your Lord and Savior? Relating your journey might finally make the whole idea of God real for them.

Now, you don't have to go through every sordid detail. Your teenager doesn't need to hear about the nasty choices you made when you were their age. But you can hint at some of your vices and sins. Kids are amazed when they consider that Dad once walked in their shoes. If you were always a pretty decent kid, your story can be even more powerful. Talk about how you thought you could do life alone, but the truth eventually sank in.

Finally, if you think that twentysomething you love so much is a lost cause, please don't give up. Instead, be thoughtful, prayerful, and intentional.

First, don't beat yourself up.

Second, think back to their life sitting beside you in a pew or that season in which they were active in youth group. What kind of spiritual turning points might they have experienced? Did they ever sincerely turn their life over to Christ? Was there a solid season when God's Spirit was leading them?

Third, keep praying, keep an open door, and trust that God will be faithful in drawing your child back to him.

If your son or daughter has never accepted Christ as Savior, then pray even harder—pray for Christian peers and mentors to come into their life, and work to keep your family relationships strong. Badgering and harping won't help. Humbly letting them see God making a difference in your life will.

Be a Sparring Partner

I can do everything through Christ, who gives me strength.
PHILIPPIANS 4:13 NLT

ave you ever boxed? Probably not.

If you have an older teenage son in good physical shape and have the kind of relationship that can survive a boxing match, maybe you should go for it. Seek out a gym where you can rent gloves and headgear and—just like in the movies—step into the ring and pretend you're in a championship bout. Bounce around the ring. Size each other up. Look for openings. Jab, cross, hook, uppercut. No punching below the belt. No nasty trash talk. The goal is for both of you to experience something you've never done before and come out winners.

Now, I know 98 percent of dads would never step into a boxing ring with one of their kids. Still, the strategy is valid. In a safe, controlled environment, do something with your maturing son or daughter that neither of you have ever experienced. From camel riding to skydiving to square dancing. Take some cuts in a batting cage. Sit at a potter's wheel. Zip down a zip line. Participate in a trivia contest. Rent a tandem bicycle. Paddle a kayak. Take a Segway tour. Play disc golf. Go through the local community college or park district catalog and pick something the two of you can do for the very first time—together.

It's not a competition. It's sharing an experience. And making a memory. Remember how you watched your toddler learn something new every day? Ask yourself, *What can I do with my older child this week to experience something new together?*

Sound the Rallying Cry

A word fitly spoken
is like apples of gold in a setting of silver.
PROVERBS 25:11 ESV

For years, I collected quotes on fathering. From Mark Twain, Winston Churchill, Dave Barry, and so on. On many occasions, I found them to be inspiring, challenging, and worthy reminders of the tasks we have as leaders of our families.

Then I got inspired to write a few of my own. See if any of these adages and thought starters resonate with you. Feel free to take ownership, write them on sticky notes, burn them onto wood plaques, or share them on social media.

> No matter where they go, what they do, or who they become, make sure your children always carry with them a little piece of home.

> The best gift a father can give to a child is himself.

> Most men have an adventure they imagined when they were growing up but never took. Children are the perfect excuse for taking it now.

> One of the best ways to get your kids talking is to share one of your own challenges and sincerely ask their advice.

> It's probably a good thing we dads can no longer sit in a La-Z-Boy chair with our pipe and slippers and hide behind the evening newspaper.

> In any crisis, a dad needs to take a breath and then say, "I love you. It'll be okay. We'll get through this together."

The best way to help single moms is to create fewer of them.

Take it from a dad who knows: Don't be the jerk in the stands.

When parents watch their child climb a tree, the first one to say, "That's high enough," is almost always Mom.

Any dad who isn't sure how to connect with his kids might consider doing what moms do.

A teenager's job is to test the waters of adulthood. A dad's job to make sure they don't get in over their head or swept off by the current.

Every day, fathers have the chance to delight or to disappoint. Choose wisely.

Every kid's first hero is their father. It's up to you to keep earning the title in every season of life.

75

Take a Stand

As for me and my house, we will serve the LORD.
JOSHUA 24:15 NASB

Remember the first time you saw this verse? Maybe on a plaque or wall hanging. For me, I instantly appreciated the confident affirmation of this short declaration. Years ago, I wasn't sure of the exact context, but I identified with Joshua's heart: "I can't speak for you or anyone else, but on behalf of my family, I am taking a stand."

You know the story. Moses had led the Israelites out of Egypt, carried the Ten Commandments down from Mt. Sinai, and wandered in the desert for 40 years but didn't quite make it into the Promised Land. He turned that privilege over to his handpicked successor, Joshua. The military strategist led God's people across the Jordan River, tumbled the walls of Jericho, conquered a long list of kings, and won back the entire Promised Land of Canaan.

In the last chapter of the book of the Bible that bears his name, Joshua called this next generation of Israelites to the city of Shechem for a final farewell. He chose this spot because that's where God had promised the land to Abraham some 400 years earlier. Speaking to the crowd, Joshua recalled the historic events that led up to this moment and proved God's faithfulness. And then he offered this challenge:

> Now, therefore, fear the LORD and serve Him in sincerity and truth; and put away the gods which your fathers served beyond the River and in Egypt, and serve the LORD. If it is disagreeable in your sight to serve the LORD, choose for yourselves today whom you will serve: whether the gods which your fathers served which were beyond the River, or

the gods of the Amorites in whose land you are living; but as for me and my house, we will serve the Lord" (Joshua 24:14-15 nasb).

In the passage, Joshua confirmed that everyone in the crowd that day had a choice to make—as do we. There are many gods. No one can make the choice for you. But there's little doubt you will serve somebody.

Joshua acknowledged that family patriarchs often choose the wrong gods. Here in the twenty-first century, those gods might include a high-profile career, sports teams, alcohol, sex, music, hot cars, high-tech gadgets, fantasy football, a lake house, or the greenest lawn on the block. It may be useful to consider what gods your own father once revered. As a dad, your god might even be having the smartest, best-behaved, most athletic kids in town.

In the end, Joshua takes a stand. He rejects all other gods and speaks for himself and his family. "As for me and my house, we will serve the Lord." It's worth remembering that one day each of Joshua's children and their children would be faced with the same choice.

Be assured, when a man makes a confident declaration to serve the Creator of the universe, he has set the stage for future generations to do the same.

76

See the Silhouette

The father of godly children has cause for joy.
PROVERBS 23:24 NLT

You're a dedicated father. You study your kids. You know how they think, what motivates them, what frightens them, and how to make them laugh. You even know how they stand, walk, jog, and run.

If you've been watching your son or daughter play an outdoor sport for a season or two, you've experienced this. You're walking from the parking lot toward the playing field—soccer, baseball, softball, lacrosse, field hockey, track, football—and you're still more than a hundred yards away. The entire team is warming up. You can't see uniform numbers. You can't see faces. From that distance, there's no way anyone could possibly distinguish one player from another.

But you can. You know your kid. The way they move, the way they stretch, the way they interact with their teammates. Your memory and their silhouette match. And you smile. That's your kid, and it doesn't matter if they play every minute or ride the bench the entire game—your love runs deep and your commitment is absolute.

Of course, you just saw them this morning. You told them you were looking forward to the game and would try to get to the field on time. Seeing them was not exactly a surprise. But still, there's that moment of satisfaction knowing that you and your family are represented by that young man or young woman wearing that jersey on this field today.

There's no lesson here. Except that seeing the silhouette is something great dads do.

77

Recognize Responsible Comedy

*There is a time for everything…
a time to weep and a time to laugh.*
ECCLESIASTES 3:1,4

Generating laughter as a family is one of life's great blessings. *But not always.* Kids—and dads—need to learn the difference.

Examples of life-affirming humor are the silly joke books for kids they sell at grade-school fund-raisers and truck-stop book racks. Look for jokes like this:

Q: Why did the chicken cross the playground?
A: To get to the other slide.

A clever dad will use laughter to help defuse an uncomfortable situation. When your two middle schoolers are arguing about what TV program to watch, you could insist they switch over to the Barney the purple dinosaur marathon. When your seventeen-year-old daughter whines that her car (which you bought for her) isn't swanky enough, reminisce how you walked ten miles to school in the snow, uphill both ways. When your seven-year-old won't eat his asparagus, grab a stalk from your plate and challenge him to a fencing duel. Loser must finish his veggies.

Other moments of family humor might emerge at unexpected moments. Such as when your son makes the perfect baloney and cheese sandwich and the dog snarfs it off the kitchen counter. That's funny, right?

Or when your teenage daughter comes into the family room to show off her new designer top…and Mom is wearing the exact same one. Funny, right?

When the baby burps at the dinner table, it's okay to laugh. But when the older kids replicate the sound, not so much.

Which brings us full circle to this idea. What is funny to some isn't necessarily funny to all. And you can't get mad when someone's sense of humor is different from yours.

Let's admit that humor can go too far. Sarcasm. Backhanded compliments. Threats about selling kids to the circus. Hiding their favorite stuffed animal. And of course, teasing about things like acne, weight, body odor, and puberty is off limits. And please never tease a girl about her hair.

Children learn to process jokes at different ages and will respond differently depending on what's going on in their lives. A wisecrack may be fine one day but backfire if the child is stressing about a homework assignment, a friend moving away, SAT testing, or a romantic entanglement.

Maybe one clue dads need to learn and can teach to their children is this: If you find yourself frequently having to say, "I was only kidding!" it might be that you tend to go too far.

Another way to test your humor is to ask yourself, *Does what I am about to say have a victim?* If so, maybe zip your lip.

There's always a chance that a younger child will not get your humor, so why risk it? Maybe worse, older kids may *understand* your joke, and it may cut them deeply.

So teach and practice responsible comedy. As for me, I have a pretty thick skin. Feel free to track me down at jaypayleitner.com and give me a nice dig, mock my receding hairline, or share your favorite not-too-naughty joke.

Deconstruct Proverbs 22:6

Train up a child in the way he should go,
even when he is old he will not depart from it.
PROVERBS 22:6 NASB

This has to be the most frequently quoted parenting verse in the Bible. And it's jam-packed with great insight. Let's take a closer look.

Proverbs 22:6 confirms that children can and should be trained. We don't let them wander recklessly through life doing whatever they think is right.

It also suggests that each child is an individual. They have their own gifts and abilities, given by the Creator. Which means that God has a reasonable, customized plan for their life, a plan that makes perfect use of all they bring to the table.

It reveals that lessons learned early have staying power. So we need to start young and teach them eternal truths that have long-term value.

It reminds us that children grow older and leave the nest. We won't always be around to guide, rescue, or protect them. As adults, they will be responsible for their own choices. That's okay because there's a good chance our training will stick with them.

Bible scholars suggest the book of Proverbs is filled with general principles, not guarantees. Still, this 21-word passage sounds like something we should take to heart.

Finally, I recommend you allow this short verse to draw you into reading all of Proverbs. Or at least chapter 22. There, in context, you'll find solid biblical advice about keeping a good name, generosity, the drawbacks of being a sluggard or deadbeat, and the advantages of learning to be skilled at your work.

Read it today. Maybe with your kids.

Think Magnificent Thoughts

*Finally, brothers and sisters, whatever is true, whatever
is noble, whatever is right, whatever is pure, whatever is
lovely, whatever is admirable—if anything is excellent or
praiseworthy—think about such things. Whatever you have
learned or received or heard from me, or seen in me—put
it into practice. And the God of peace will be with you.*

PHILIPPIANS 4:8-9

Are you as angry as I am that working professionals are creating tons and tons of garbage out there and calling it art?

A vast array of today's so-called entertainment is violent, depressing, graphic, filthy, angry, and devoid of hope. Every generation seems to sink to a new level of what they consider acceptable in mainstream books, movies, art, and music. Even worse than the obvious assault on our senses may be the subtle systematic perversion of our worldview. In the name of tolerance, any choice made by anyone at any time is not to be judged.

But frankly, we shouldn't be surprised. Protecting morality is not the responsibility of film studios, network executives, publishers, or music producers. They are just doing their job. Their assignment is to make as much money as possible for their companies. If they don't believe in God, why would they follow a biblical worldview when pushing their products to the marketplace? And by the way, these professionals are very good at what they do.

With that in mind, Dad, you need something beyond your own opinion to convince your son or daughter that there is a better option than filling their minds with garbage, lies, and half-truths.

The answer may be found in the above passage from Philippians.

For as long as our kids are under our influence, let's help them to evaluate the things they read, listen to, or watch through the reliable filter of Scripture. Have them consider, *Is this piece of art or literature noble, pure, lovely, admirable, excellent, and praiseworthy?* If they do that, the God of peace will be with them.

So how do you find and introduce them to art that is noble and true? This century, it takes creativity, research, and follow-through. The great artists of centuries past dedicated their work to the One who gave them creativity. Think of the God-honoring music and art of the Renaissance. The word "magnificent" comes to mind. Unfortunately, most of today's artists, musicians, and filmmakers are motivated by other gods.

A dad needs to read reviews of movies, music, and books. Talk to other parents. Be a student of the culture. We need to invest a little time and money to take our sons and daughters to fine art galleries and uplifting concerts. Help them fall in love with classic literature from authors like C.S. Lewis, J.R.R. Tolkien, and Jane Austen. That's not to say older is necessarily better. Many contemporary creatives are quite inspiring. You may need to explore outside the cultural mainstream. Also, you don't have to limit yourself to Christian artists, producers, and publishers, but that's a pretty good place to start.

80

Miss Your Kids

Words from the mouth of a wise man are gracious,
while the lips of a fool consume him.
ECCLESIASTES 10:12 NASB

If you're in that stage of life when kids are constantly underfoot, you may not fully appreciate this concept. But sometime in the future, you will miss having your kids around. Really.

During their teen years, they will choose to spend time someplace other than your home. That includes the basement, backyard, or lakeside cottage of a high-school friend. Also, youth retreats, sports camps, and mission trips. As well as college visits, slumber parties, and weekends with out-of-state cousins.

Before they head off, you'll want to confirm that all these events have responsible adult supervision. Other than that, you pretty much need to let them go. They're not abandoning you. It's good for teens to leave the nest once in a while on a trial run.

Still, you'll want to stay in tune with your gut instincts regarding how, when, and why they are keeping their distance. Ask yourself, *Is this simply a healthy physical separation? Or is it emotional? Or even spiritual?*

If you are seeing less and less of your maturing teen, don't panic, but do listen to your own heart. Is your son or daughter missing family functions they once enjoyed? When they are home, is the air filled with tension and terse words? Please don't insist they make every family function and stay from beginning to end. Don't make accusations or point fingers. Instead, admit that something is getting in the way.

Start by making sure your home is a place where love lives. When they walk in, welcome them. You're glad they're here, right? When they leave, wish them well without heaping on any guilt about leaving too soon or by trying to schedule the next visit.

When your young adult children are under your roof for a day or a season, judge less and celebrate more. Focus on the joy of the moment. Make them glad to be with you. And eager to come back.

If you haven't seen them for a while, you may think there's a problem, but it may be just the busyness of life. It's easy for young people who truly love their parents to go for weeks or months without initiating contact. You may feel some kind of tension, but it may all be in your imagination.

So, Dad, don't wait until things get weird. In general, the longer it's been, the more awkward the conversation. It might be up to you to take the initiative, pick up the phone, and say something like, "Hey, I miss you. Can I buy you lunch sometime next week?" Or "Mom and I are thinking about taking a road trip to see you. What's your calendar look like?"

Is that something you need to do? Find the words and then make the call or send the text.

81

Do Teachable Moments

Be careful never to forget what you yourself have seen. Do not let these memories escape from your mind as long as you live! And be sure to pass them on to your children and grandchildren.

DEUTERONOMY 4:9 NLT

'm pretty sure that as a devoted dad, you already take full advantage of teachable moments. You know the idea. It's all about passing on your wisdom and experience while you're doing life together. Examples?

- Walking in the woods and seeing poison ivy is when you teach about avoiding it. ("Leaflets three, let it be.")

- When you get a flat tire, you take the extra time to teach your son or daughter about pulling far off the road onto a level space, positioning the jack correctly, tightening lug nuts in the proper sequence, and so on.

- When the power goes out, you grab the good flashlight and the nearest kids so they can learn how a fuse box works. They also realize that to find the good flashlight in the dark, they need to always put it back in the same strategic location.

- At the post office, you teach kids to make wise choices regarding cost versus speed of delivery, and you explain how planning ahead can save rush delivery charges.

- When you're watching an innocent TV show and two unmarried folks suddenly jump in the sack, you turn to your middle schooler and say, "You know that's not how God designed it, right?"

- Taking your kids grocery shopping leads to all kinds of teachable moments: picking out a ripe cantaloupe, respecting other shoppers, practicing math skills, and not believing shocking tabloid headlines.

Teachable moments bring fresh value to mundane chores or momentary frustrations. When you take time to include a warning or explain the hows and the whys, activities may take a little longer. This may also require a bit of thought and intentionality. But that's what you signed up for when you became a dad. The unmistakable benefit is that your kids are learning life strategies and developing decision-making skills that will serve them well for years to come.

82

Do Prayable Moments

Rejoice always, pray continually, give thanks in all
circumstances; for this is God's will for you in Christ Jesus.
1 THESSALONIANS 5:16-18

What's better than teachable moments? Prayable moments.
Examples?

- You and your little guy or gal are doing chalk pictures on the sidewalk, and you hear a siren several blocks away. Stop and pray. You don't know the details of that emergency, but God does.

- You're stuck in a slight traffic jam on the way to school, church, a concert, or a sporting event. Turn off the car radio and pray that no matter when you get there, God will be honored in the upcoming event.

- A storm front is moving in. Pray for the safety of your family and your neighbors.

- You pass a church where wedding guests are throwing rice at a bride and groom, or you pass a car with a Just Married sign. That's a fun prayable moment. Offer a prayer for those newlyweds and add a prayer of thanks for your own spouse.

- Through social media, radio, TV, or whatever, you find out about a breaking national or international news event. Whether it's good news or bad news, stop for a moment with your kids and express thanks to God that he is in control.

Prayable moments are nothing new to you. When you experience a need or see God working, you very likely offer a prayer of supplication or thanksgiving. You may even be moved to give glory to God when you see a beautiful sunset, encounter his power in a thunderstorm, or experience a personal revelation of joy. But most of those prayers are done in silence and don't include your kids. And, Dad, that's a lost opportunity.

Next time you're just hanging out with your kids, be on the lookout for moments large and small that are worthy of prayer. They're not hard to find. One of the great benefits of prayable moments is that they give your children a view of the world beyond themselves. You're helping them become thoughtful, caring, and praying adults.

83

Explain Syzygy

When I consider your heavens, the work of your fingers, the moon and the stars, which you have set in place, what is mankind that you are mindful of them, human beings that you care for them?

PSALM 8:3-4

When they were barely sitting up, you could amaze your son or daughter with a simple game of peekaboo. At six or seven, you bought a globe, and they finally understood the difference between states, countries, and continents. A few years later, you had them spellbound as you explained how to make the perfect s'more, what the infield fly rule is, how to castle in chess, and where babies come from.

But as they get older, you know fewer and fewer things that they don't. Or at least that's what they think.

So to help keep you one step ahead, it's time to teach you something so you can teach it to them. I'm 99 percent sure your teenager does not know the very cool-looking word "syzygy."

Syzygy (pronounced SIH-zih-jee) is the scientific term for the alignment of three celestial bodies in a gravitational system. The most obvious examples of that are a solar and lunar eclipse. Now listen carefully; there will be a test.

A *solar* eclipse occurs when the moon sneaks between the earth and the sun, blocking out some or most of the sun's rays for a short period of time. A solar eclipse happens during the day, and if it's a total eclipse, it will bring virtual darkness to a path as wide as 70 miles. A solar eclipse comes with warnings not to look directly at the sun. (Note to dads: Those warnings will actually tempt kids to peek at the sun.)

A *lunar* eclipse occurs when the earth passes between the sun and the moon, casting an obvious shadow on the surface of the moon. Please don't confuse the relatively rare lunar eclipse with the monthly lunar cycle, during which you see new moons, quarter moons, half-moons, and full moons.

Just to be absolutely clear, there is no time when the sun passes between the earth and the moon. If for no other reason, it wouldn't fit. On average, the moon is 238,857 miles away, and the diameter of the sun is 864,938 miles.

Syzygy of the sun, moon, and earth may occur a few times a year. Dads who track such astronomical phenomena on the NASA website and make sure their kids understand what's going on are true heroes.

Here's the point: You want your children to learn things you don't know. You want them to think big thoughts and pursue big dreams beyond your imagination. But it's comforting and inspiring for children of any age to experience authentic and fascinating teachable moments from their father.

It goes back to that idea that we all need to have confidence in who we are and where we came from. Dad, your kids may *act* smart, but deep down they need to know that you *are* smart.

Hold Your Baby

You created my inmost being; you knit me together in my mother's
womb. I praise you because I am fearfully and wonderfully
made; your works are wonderful, I know that full well. My
frame was not hidden from you when I was made in the secret
place, when I was woven together in the depths of the earth.
Your eyes saw my unformed body; all the days ordained for me
were written in your book before one of them came to be.

PSALM 139:13-16

By the time we brought our first baby home from the hospital, Alec had already spent two weeks in a neonatal intensive care unit. He's perfectly healthy now. But for his first week of life, it was a little scary. That's when Rita vowed that if she had the chance, she would hold him and not let him go.

What a gift that has been. In short order, Rita mastered the art of doing everything she had to do with one arm while holding a newborn with the other. It's an impressive skill. Decades later, Rita has invested thousands of hours swaddling five of our own kids, ten foster babies, scores of babies in church nurseries, and six grandbabies. Plus, she's encouraged and taught dozens of other young moms and dads to do the same.

In this book—listing things great dads do—I encourage you not to leave baby-holding to Mom. She may be better at it than you. You may even be initially uncomfortable or even fearful of holding a newborn who seems so fragile. But push through any hesitation and be the dad your new baby needs.

Never Expect Quality Time to Make Up for Lost Quantity Time

Your wife will be like a fruitful vine within your house;
your children will be like olive shoots around your table.

PSALM 128:3

The debate is over. The expert consensus is that you really cannot expect to have any quality time with your children unless you have sufficient quantity time. The idea that we can work 70-hour weeks, ignore our kids month after month, and then make up for it with a trip to Disney World or a long weekend skiing at Aspen is a myth. Your kids may have fun in Orlando or Colorado, but it won't be with you. It will be with a stranger who happens to know their name and pay the bills.

Is that harsh? A little. Naturally, there may be a season of life when your job takes you away from your family for an uncomfortable number of minutes, hours, days, or weeks. It doesn't have to spell disaster. My advice is to minimize that time away, prepare to make any difficult career decisions that need to be made, and have long, heartfelt talks with your bride about what's best for the family.

Finally, when you do get a chance to get away as a family, steer clear of ambitious, frantic vacations where everyone gets a little tense and testy. Although you can never reclaim time lost, you can make the most of the time you do have. Take trips that allow plenty of time to discover the quiet beauty of God's creation and rediscover your family.

Like my friend Josh McDowell says, "To a kid, 'love' is spelled T-I-M-E."

Call, Text, or Reach Out
to Them Right Now

Which of you, if your son asks for bread, will give him a stone? Or if
he asks for a fish, will give him a snake? If you, then, though you are
evil, know how to give good gifts to your children, how much more
will your Father in heaven give good gifts to those who ask him!

MATTHEW 7:9-11

When they're little, your kids believe you know everything. That idea brings comfort and security. They think, *Dad is my brilliant, perfect guide through life.*

About the time they get their first cell phone, all that changes. They begin to realize the world is a big and busy place, and Dad can't possibly have all the answers.

You're no longer superhuman, but that's okay. You're something better. A trusted resource. An honest sounding board. A sincere cheerleader. A refuge in any storm.

Older kids may not say it, but they love to hear from Dad. They love knowing you're reachable. So when you think of them, let 'em know. They're glad you are just a text, phone call, walk down the hallway, or short drive away.

It's worth noting that your effort to stay connected doesn't just strengthen their relationship with you. Christian psychologists confirm that the trust and confidence individuals have in their dad has a direct impact on the trust and confidence they have in their heavenly Father.

That's right. Communicating openly and consistently with your son or daughter just might help them develop a consistent and rich prayer life.

Prohibit Whining

What have you done to us by bringing us out of Egypt? Didn't we say to you in Egypt, "Leave us alone; let us serve the Egyptians"? It would have been better for us to serve the Egyptians than to die in the desert!
EXODUS 14:11-12

No one likes a whiner. That's one of the reasons there's a lovely plaque hanging in our kitchen that says No Whining.

Actually, I don't recall any of our kids doing a lot of whining, so I'm not sure what motivated the purchase of that piece of art. I believe it was a gift. In any case, I think I'd rather deal with sarcasm, the silent treatment, or an all-out tantrum than an afternoon of whining.

As it turns out, the Israelites were world-class whiners. In this real-life scenario from Exodus, the Israelites whining to Moses are facing death from the fast-approaching Egyptian army, so maybe we should cut them some slack. Plus, they don't know that Moses is about to lead them across the dry bottom of the Red Sea in the greatest escape in history. But they *should* know. Or at least they should trust. God always has a plan. Quite often, it's more surprising and more satisfying than anything you could ever imagine.

So here are four quick antidotes for whining. One, remind your kids how good they have it. Two, take away the luxury item that triggered the whining—the phone that isn't the latest model or the dinner plate with the vegetables they don't like. Three, call the family together and read the chapters in Exodus that feature those unbelievably whiny Israelites. Four, get your own No Whining sign.

Counteract the Smartphone Crisis

Do not conform to the pattern of this world, but be transformed by the renewing of your mind. Then you will be able to test and approve what God's will is—his good, pleasing and perfect will.

ROMANS 12:2

Which of these activities defined your youth? Going to the mall. Traveling sports. Summer camp. Church activities. Going to the beach. Skateboarding. Hanging out under streetlamps. Riding buses. Street hockey. Riding bikes around the neighborhood. Getting your driver's license. Chores. A part-time job. Helping with the family business. Cruising up and down Main Street.

All these things involved a lot of interaction with other people— out of the house and face-to-face. Some activities may have been more edifying and beneficial than others. Some took athleticism, some took brains, some took brawn, some required ingenuity. But clearly, what you did in your youth laid groundwork for who you are today.

What about your preteen or teenager? According to the word on the street and more than a few blogs, your son's or daughter's life may very well be characterized by lying in bed with their phone in their hand, texting, gaming, Snapchatting, sending and receiving selfies, using the latest dating app, or employing other social media.

Extended periods of this kind of activity seem fraught with danger. Perhaps even signaling a crisis in the making.

Every kid is unique, but repercussions might include a reduced attention span, family disconnect, sleep deprivation, depression, lack of exercise, inhibited interpersonal communication skills, and a desperate need for an attitude adjustment.

One of the great ironies is that the most powerful personal

communication device in the history of the world may be causing kids to feel more isolated. Not to mention the possibility that unrestricted and unmonitored use of social media may open the doors to sexting, identity theft, bullying, being bullied, and engaging unknowingly with sexual predators.

Maybe it's not all that bad. New research on teens and smartphones seems to come out every few months. And experts disagree on the severity of the problem and how parents should respond. While banning smartphones is probably not an option, delaying their inevitable usage is probably a good idea. When your kids start asking for one, let them know you'll discuss it with your child's mom and get back to them. Then say, "We're thinking it might be a couple more years." Prepare for some unpleasant feedback.

When it comes to technology, you have a responsibility to protect your son or daughter from as many negative consequences as possible. And even if "everyone has one!" that doesn't mean your kids have to have one.

Finally, that list you pondered at the opening of this chapter was more than just a trip down memory lane. It's a reminder that life can exist without smartphones, and you have a personal history to prove it. There really are all kinds of activities that just might get them up, out of bed, off their phones, and interacting with real life

Even if it's just hanging out under streetlamps or cruising Main Street. Hey, you survived.

Discover Shadows

*Every good and perfect gift is from above, coming
down from the Father of the heavenly lights, who
does not change like shifting shadows.*
JAMES 1:17

Have you ever been with a two-year-old when they discover their shadow? It's amusing and amazing. On a sunny day, they suddenly see and recognize the shape of their hand on the sidewalk. They point to their hand as their hand moves. They stand still to see if their shadow does the same. Then they try to step on that two-dimensional outline of themselves. They jump and squeal and learn.

Dad, you can be the one to show them. Look for that chance right around their second birthday.

If your kids are a little older, you can still have fun with shadows. Note that at high noon, midsummer shadows are almost nonexistent. But on a midwinter morning or evening, the angle of the sun is much lower, and shadows stretch for half a block.

Inside, a single light source allows for all sorts of shadow lessons. An object close to the wall leaves a shadow about the size of the object. But move that plastic army man or dinosaur close to the light source, and the shadow fills the wall. Of course, shadow puppets will never go out of style. I recommend you initially try forming a bunny, barking dog, and butterfly.

With your bored teenager, share this empowering fact: When they stand in the sun, their shadow confirms that light has traveled nearly 93 million miles *unobstructed*, only to be deprived of reaching the ground in the final few feet thanks to their presence.

Expect Sin

Love covers a multitude of sins.

1 PETER 4:8 NASB

Dads mess up. At least I do. And I have a sneaking suspicion you do too. The chance for men in our culture to fall into a puddle, pool, or ocean of sin is 100 percent. A brief review of the seven deadly sins is enough to convict us and remind us that we are far, far, far from perfect. For the record, we're looking at greed, slothfulness, envy, wrath, pride, lust, or gluttony. When you sift through that list, which one do you park on? Pride tends to bust my chops more and more these days. The other six aren't far behind.

Thankfully, love covers not just seven sins, but a multitude of sins. The above verse from 1 Peter is referring to God's grace. The idea is that God knows us and loves us. He knows our shortcomings and imperfections. He even expects them. Yes, he's disappointed in our sins. They break his heart. But still, nothing we do can ever separate us from his perfect love.

Is there a lesson in there someplace for dads? Probably several.

For ourselves: We need to acknowledge our own sinful condition. Flee the world's carnality. Constantly ask God for help. Be broken before him, knowing we can rest in his grace.

For our kids: As fathers, we should absolutely make sure our children understand the idea that God loves each of us unconditionally, which means we can go to him with confidence. He wants us to surrender our brokenness to him, ask forgiveness, and accept the gift of Jesus's sacrifice on our behalf. Then, as parents, we can model a similar kind of grace in our own relationship with our children. Let your kids know that nothing they could ever do would cause you to love them any less.

Strive to know and understand what your kids are going through. Expect them to make mistakes. Be disappointed sometimes. But never let anything get in the way of your unconditional love.

To be sure, sins, mistakes, flubs, and screwups often come with some fallout and kickback. Love doesn't necessarily make those repercussions go away. We often have to pay the penalty for our sins here on earth. That's a good thing; that's how we learn. But in the long run—in eternity—it all works out for good to those who are called according to God's purpose.

Before leaving this topic, a question all fathers should be asking is, "Who am I tougher on—my kids or myself?" Some of us need to begin holding ourselves to a higher standard and then get serious about leading our family to a life of brokenness, surrender, and new life in Christ. On the other hand, some stern and judgmental dads need to practice giving a little grace of their own. Which means taking a breath, cutting their kids some slack, and enjoying their family just a little more.

91

Invite Them into Your World

May your deeds be shown to your servants,
your splendor to their children.
May the favor of the Lord our God rest on us;
establish the work of our hands for us—
yes, establish the work of our hands.
PSALM 90:16-17

I don't know anything about quantum physics. But if I were a quantum physicist, I would definitely teach my kids something about quantum physics.

I have never attempted calf roping. But if it were my passion, I would certainly invite my kids to my next rodeo.

I am a writer and speaker, so my kids regularly see me at my keyboard, read the things I write (especially if it's about them), and sometimes sneak into the back of an auditorium to listen to me blah, blah, blah about parenting, marriage, finding your life purpose, and so on.

Whatever you do and whoever you are, I challenge you to give your children numerous opportunities to enter your world. Especially when it comes to your career, passions, hobbies, and life skills. Not so they'll follow your footsteps. More so, because kids want and need to know a little about their old man.

We all know butcher shops, dry cleaners, construction companies, and car dealerships that have been in the same family for generations. My dentist's daughter is a dentist. Tim Sheehan and Claire Sheehan share an office just down the street.

"Should I do what Dad does?" is a question that all growing kids will consider for at least a day or two. My dad was an elementary-school principal, and for about two minutes I considered a career in education.

In like manner, your kids should have a reasonable answer when people ask, "What does your dad do?" When my son Max was about six, someone asked him that question. Max knew I had an office in our home and had seen me wander out several times a day for stretch and snack breaks. His reply was, "He eats apples."

Do your kids know what you do? Ask them. You may be surprised at the answer.

Finally, because one of your jobs is to help equip your children for the future, consider this scenario. When your son or daughter stands up to say a few words at your funeral, will they be left mumbling something like, "I never really knew what my dad did...or who he was...or what he cared about." Dad, please don't let that happen.

Which leads to this question: What will you say about your own father while standing next to his casket? Which leads to this reasonable challenge: If he's still around, are there traits and achievements you might further uncover and still add to that little speech?

92

Endow Your Kids with Roots and Wings

*Do nothing out of selfish ambition or vain conceit. Rather, in
humility value others above yourselves, not looking to your
own interests but each of you to the interests of the others.*

PHILIPPIANS 2:3-4

Imagine your son or daughter coming to you with a slightly crazy idea. To sell vintage comic books online. To start a harmonica band. To raise salamanders. To quit school and design apps for a living. To write a Broadway show based on a Bible story, classic novel, or Revolutionary War hero.

Is your first impulse to throw up warnings and roadblocks? Or would you listen, nod your head, and say, "Wow. That's fantastic. How can I help?"

One of the great joys of fathering is watching a child pursue a dream. To find a passion. To throw themselves 100 percent into a project or cause. To set high goals. To pursue excellence.

That's all good, right?

Well, yes. Except that—as big as their dreams are—there is something bigger. We all need to pursue and follow God's calling in our life. Knowing him and pursuing his plan is the only true source of fulfillment and contentment. It's about trusting that he is enough. He is all we need.

This dilemma describes perhaps the great challenge of fatherhood. To encourage our kids to reach for the stars, but also to make sure they know that putting God first is the primary goal and it's really okay if they *don't* become world famous, fabulously wealthy, and supremely powerful.

A dad can't possibly do both at the same time, can he? Push his kids to do great things...while submitting to God?

Simply put, the goal is to do *both*. Do great things *for* God. Excellence with humility. Giving credit to their Creator for their success.

Some might call it servant leadership. That's what Jesus demonstrated at the Last Supper when he washed the feet of his disciples *and* laid out the plan for saving the world.

Servant leadership is what happens when you strive for excellence in a pursuit that directly builds the kingdom of God. That includes pastoring, teaching Sunday school, writing devotionals and Bible studies, and traveling across the world to evangelize the lost. But it could be following a calling that doesn't immediately look like "ministry."

For some people, servant leadership might actually mean becoming famous, wealthy, and powerful while giving all the glory to God. (That's not easy. But it is possible.)

Another way to describe this idea is giving your kids roots and wings. Help them build a foundation of love, respect, humility, reverence, and biblical literacy—roots. From that sturdy platform, launch them with creativity, confidence, wisdom, discernment, and vision—wings.

Go ahead and give your blessing to whatever your kids identify as their true passion. They can raise salamanders, write a musical, or start a harmonica band. Or even be wealthy and world famous. All to the glory of God.

93

Watch Your Words

Fathers, do not embitter your children, or
they will become discouraged.
COLOSSIANS 3:21

'm pro-dad. The last thing I want to do is make any father feel cruddy or filled with regrets. But we can't publish a book about what great dads do without admitting that sometimes we blow it. We embitter our children, and they become discouraged.

Often, we do it with our words. We slide a clever sarcastic remark across the dinner table. We chastise our kids for behavior we've been modeling for years. We set expectations that are beyond their capabilities or far different from their hopes and dreams. We make a correction and then make it again, again, and again without giving them time to process it. We degrade them in front of their friends.

Discouraging words slip out so easily. Here's an example that might hit close to home. It does for me. Through extra effort and determination, a young person makes an improvement in a field of study, athletics, creative arts, or other worthwhile pursuit. With a justifiable hint of pride, they tell us about it. What do we do? Instead of congratulating or celebrating, we give off a vibe or even use words that say, "It's about time," or "Of course—I would expect nothing less."

Often, when we're trying to do the right thing as fathers, that's exactly when we push too hard or say too much.

As with so many biblical admonitions, it's helpful to turn this one upside down. Allow me to paraphrase Colossians 3:21. "Dads, speak encouragement to kids and allow them to chase their dreams, and they will become courageous and empowered."

94

Pray a Blessing

Jesus came from Galilee to the Jordan to be baptized by John. But John tried to deter him, saying, "I need to be baptized by you, and do you come to me?" Jesus replied, "Let it be so now; it is proper for us to do this to fulfill all righteousness." Then John consented. As soon as Jesus was baptized, he went up out of the water. At that moment heaven was opened, and he saw the Spirit of God descending like a dove and alighting on him. And a voice from heaven said, "This is my Son, whom I love; with him I am well pleased."

MATTHEW 3:13-17

This familiar scene introduces us to Jesus as an adult at the very beginning of his world-changing three-year public ministry. In the next chapter he will spend 40 days being tempted in the desert and then handpick his 12-man posse.

But first he gets baptized by John and blessed by his Father. In that blessing you'll find a few things great dads can do.

First, speak words. Some dads are the strong, silent type. But when it comes to your children, the verbal expression of your love is something they cannot hear enough.

Second, sometimes go a little overboard. God made the heavens open and sent a dove to represent himself. What can you do—once in a while—to speak publicly into the life of your child?

Third, confirm your unconditional love. God sees all time and space at the same moment. When he says, "This is my Son, whom I love," that commitment is now, always, and forever.

Fourth—and this is actually pretty stunning—Jesus had not yet begun his earthly ministry. He really had not done *anything* yet. Still God was well pleased with his Son. Is it possible that we can tell our sons and daughters we are proud to be their father even when they haven't done anything awesome recently?

Dad, do this. No matter who they are or what they've accomplished, turn to God and dedicate your son or daughter to his service and glory. Give your blessing. And ask for God's blessing.

It could be a one-time event on their thirteenth birthday. Or maybe pray over them every fall as you send them off to school. Or offer a blessing every night when you tuck them in.

I know parents who have orchestrated a significant rite of passage to mark their child's entry into adulthood. You may want to present your son or daughter with a token gift to mark the occasion: a ring, a Bible, a sword, a necklace, a letter, a set of car keys, or a pony. (Probably not a pony.)

If a one-time event sounds like something you want to initiate, don't hesitate. If you wait for the right moment to work out every detail, it may never happen. Pick a date on the calendar. No excuses.

Day after day, we watch our little boys and girls grow, but one day soon we will turn around with amazement to see they have become men and women. Make sure each of your precious children experience your blessing.

95

Watch the Horizon

While he was still a long way off, his father saw him coming.
LUKE 15:20 NLT

M ight you have a prodigal? That would be a son or daughter who has stormed off, snuck away, or left home in such a way that they no longer feel welcome.

That's hard. And not uncommon.

Every situation is different, but my recommendation is to leave the light on. Let them know they are always welcome. With all the technology available, you should be able to communicate that idea to them wherever they are. Then pray for them. Don't give up. Keep living your own life. Working, dreaming, loving, learning. But watch the horizon.

You know the well-loved parable, but you may not have thought too much about that moment when the father sees the unmistakable figure of his youngest son approaching from a distance. Here's how Jesus begins the parable:

> A man had two sons. The younger son told his father, "I want my share of your estate now before you die." So his father agreed to divide his wealth between his sons.
>
> A few days later this younger son packed all his belongings and moved to a distant land, and there he wasted all his money in wild living. About the time his money ran out, a great famine swept over the land, and he began to starve. He persuaded a local farmer to hire him, and the man sent him into his fields to feed the pigs. The young man became so hungry that even the pods he was feeding the pigs looked good to him. But no one gave him anything.

When he finally came to his senses, he said to himself, "At
home even the hired servants have food enough to spare,
and here I am dying of hunger! I will go home to my father
and say, 'Father, I have sinned against both heaven and you,
and I am no longer worthy of being called your son. Please
take me on as a hired servant.'" So he returned home to his
father (Luke 15:11-20 NLT).

Consider what that father has been doing for all those months. He
may have been a bit perturbed when the younger son insisted on snag-
ging an early share of his inheritance. But any anger didn't last long. He
loved the boy and spent many hours worrying about him. Plus, he had
to make sure the older son—who now had twice as much work to do—
still felt appreciated. And don't forget, famine had swept the country,
and he was probably busy trying to minimize crop losses.

Through all that, he kept an eye on the horizon. Then one day he
saw a familiar figure walking hesitantly down that dusty road. When he
saw the boy, what did he do? Did he turn his back and force the boy to
grovel? Did he fold his arms and prepare to deliver a long lecture? That
father did what you would do. He ran. With arms wide open.

And while he was still a long way off, his father saw him
coming. Filled with love and compassion, he ran to his
son, embraced him, and kissed him. His son said to him,
"Father, I have sinned against both heaven and you, and I
am no longer worthy of being called your son."

But his father said to the servants, "Quick! Bring the finest
robe in the house and put it on him. Get a ring for his finger
and sandals for his feet. And kill the calf we have been fat-
tening. We must celebrate with a feast, for this son of mine
was dead and has now returned to life. He was lost, but
now he is found." So the party began (Luke 15:20-24 NLT).

Jesus finishes the story with an emotional and instructive conversation between the father and the older son. Clearly, the theological
connotations of the parable are profound. The master teacher was

providing a graphic image of God's unconditional love and confirming that no matter what you've done, God will always celebrate the day when a lost person finally surrenders to grace.

That's a huge lesson. Really, that's the entire point of the Bible, isn't it? But you're still thinking about that kid walking over the hill and his dad coming out with a big old bear hug, right?

Dad, when your children leave home—for a school day, a summer mission trip, a college semester, a tour of duty, or some "wild living"—don't ever lose sight of the horizon. Keep watching expectantly. You can do that because you've made your home a place your kids are always welcome. Pray they feel your overflowing love. Pray for their safe return. Pray for your own open arms and open heart.

The father's response throughout the entire story reminds us to be patient with our children. Your kids are going to disappoint you. They may turn their backs on you. They may squander your hard-earned money on stuff you don't approve of. The prodigal's father models how we need to watch and wait expectantly. When you first get a glimpse of that son or daughter you know so well and love so much, run to them. And get ready to party.

96

Splurge (Occasionally)

In everything I showed you that by working hard in this manner
you must help the weak and remember the words of the Lord Jesus,
that He Himself said, "It is more blessed to give than to receive."
ACTS 20:35 NASB

Raising kids ain't cheap. The most recent report from the United States Department of Agriculture calculated the costs of raising a child from birth to age 17 is $233,610.[7] And that doesn't include college. Yikes.

Now hold on. I tell you that not so you hesitate having children (or more children). I believe your kids and mine are worth every nickel. A grown-up kid for right around a quarter-million dollars? That's a bargain.

I'm sharing this report from the USDA so that you get the most for your money. That requires you to not only invest money in your kids, but to also give of yourself. That's the only way you can hope to get any kind of reasonable return on your investment. Make sense?

Which brings us to a clever strategy I came up with on how to invest time and money in your kids. Specifically, on visits to places like theme parks, zoos, county fairs, and ballparks.

I've been there. And I'm just like you. After a dad pays for parking and admission, he typically spends the rest of the day saying no to additional expenses. No to souvenirs. No to snacks. No to almost all additional surcharges. And that's okay. Really, kids need to learn they can't have everything they ask for. As a matter of fact, they need to learn to stop asking! (And whining is never permitted.)

But once in a while—before you enter the gates—announce a splurge day! Budget an extra wad of cash and let your entire family know that you intend to say yes to just about any reasonable request.

Does that idea frighten you? Dad, you may discover your kids don't go as crazy as you think. There's a good chance their choices and purchases will be thoughtful and reasonable. If it goes well, follow that up with splurges at bookstores, ice-cream shops, and thrift stores.

The best part of the occasional splurge is that you will have an easier time enforcing limits and reducing requests and whining on future visits to the park, fair, store, and zoo. You can even announce, "Hey, gang, this is not a splurge event."

Finally, if you're the kind of dad who already overindulges your kids on most family outings, try a reverse splurge. That would be going to the theme park or zoo and doing only what comes with regular admission. No sno-cones. No stuffed koalas. No extra shows. Your kids may discover they can have fun without all the extras.

Listen

He who gives an answer before he hears,
it is folly and shame to him.

PROVERBS 18:13 NASB

Here's a little test to assess your listening skills. Ask yourself, *When's the last time my child came to me with a question or problem?*

If you're not a very good listener, your children may have learned long ago not to bother you because you don't really listen anyway—all you do is lecture and then go back to what you were doing before you were interrupted.

Maybe that suits you just fine. You don't really want to be bothered by their problems and requests. But be warned. If your kids need to talk about something, they are going to find someone to talk to. They will find someone who will listen. And that person will offer advice. And it could be not-so-good advice.

It may be that listening doesn't come naturally to men. It feels like a passive activity, and we're action-oriented. The solution? Practice *active* listening. Ask questions. Nod. Make eye contact with your kids. Get clarification. Rephrase their words back to them, so they know you really heard what they're saying. Don't be too quick with answers. Make it a point to pause before giving advice. To a kid, listening equates with caring.

If you're the kind of guy who likes to lecture, it's worth noting that by listening well, your lecture will be more on target and have more impact.

By the way, listening is a good way to communicate that you care about your wife as well. But you already knew that.

Accept the Gift

Children are a gift from the LORD; they are a reward from him.
PSALM 127:3 NLT

Contrary to conventional wisdom, children are not a *burden* from the Lord. They are a *gift*. A *reward*.

Unfortunately, some fathers refuse to accept that gift. They are horrified by the idea of baby spit on their sport coat. They have no desire to dance with their young daughter in the kitchen or twenty years later at her wedding. The idea of playing catch with their son is not even on their radar. My heart breaks for those men, and I wonder what went wrong.

Research tells us disconnected fathers tend to fall into three categories.

Maybe they never had an involved, caring father, and therefore have no point of reference for the joys of fatherhood. To that man, I say, "You can be everything your father wasn't. For the sake of your own children, break that chain. Find an older father in your church or community and ask for his wise counsel. Consider the idea of opening your heart to your father-in-law. Ask God to be your Father."

Maybe those men feel trapped. Their marriage is well past the honeymoon stage and they barely know their children. To that man, I say, "Boldly invest a season of your life into surrendering to the needs of your wife and your kids. Study them. Discern what makes them laugh or cry. Make long lists of anything and everything that seems to meet their core needs and their desires. And then fulfill every one. Don't be surprised when all your sacrificial efforts come back to you one hundredfold."

Maybe those men are caught up by some worldly distraction. Work.

Drugs. Alcohol. Lust. Power. Fame. Gambling. Greed. To that man I say, "Get addicted to being a dad. Grab a hug. Tie a shoelace. Give a horsey ride. Hang out with a teen. Read ten more books like this one. Be a hero. "

All fathers, I believe, share a little of all three of the above disconnections. Even if our own father had his act together, there will always be some regrets and frustrations from our youth. All men get selfish and put ourselves first on occasion. The temptations of the world will sometimes steal our focus from our responsibilities as fathers.

But you can't beat yourself up. Indeed, there will be setbacks. We live in a fallen world and bad stuff happens. But that's when a faithful dad looks at the big picture and commits for the long haul. If you don't give up, you can overcome your past, your frustrations, and your distractions.

The answer, again, is to open your heart, mind, and soul to the gift of fatherhood. Like any awesome gift, don't just put it on a shelf. Put it to work. Play with it. Care for it. Talk about it. Show it off. Let the gift of fatherhood open your life to new possibilities and a glorious future. Enjoy.

Be a Forever Father

*For the L*ORD *is good and his love endures forever; his*
faithfulness continues through all generations.

PSALM 100:5

When is a dad no longer a dad? The answer is never.
If you've loved on a newborn, taught a five-year-old to ride
a bike, given the birds-and-bees talk, handed over car keys to
a new driver, or wandered into the empty bedroom of a son or daughter after they've moved out on their own, you are forever a dad.

And the world needs dads. Good ones like you. "Forever Fathers"
who establish a strong foundation of faith, sort out messes, protect children from nasty influences, and mold mushy young minds into clear-thinking adults.

When your kids are no longer living under your roof, their needs
have changed, but you are still a valuable part of their life. You've
bought homes, cars, and life insurance. They haven't. You've replaced
water heaters, caulked windows, and bought appliances and mattresses.
They haven't. You have a good idea about what home repairs to do yourself and when to call in a professional. You have tools they don't and
patience they need. So, just when you think your dad skills are obsolete, you're really entering an entirely new phase of your father-child
relationship.

Then, of course, just over the horizon is an entirely new season of
fathering. Just when you start getting comfortable in your empty nest,
one of two things happen. A grown kid moves back home. (Yikes!) Or
your son or daughter presents you with a third generation. And you get
a whole new name: Gramps. (Yes!)

Be an Awesome Grandpa

Grandchildren are the crowning glory of the aged;
parents are the pride of their children.
PROVERBS 17:6 NLT

With your own children, you're too busy being a dad to think about your legacy. But when your kids have kids, it changes everything. You begin to really think about how you will be remembered by future generations.

As you read this book for dads, you're not thinking about twenty years from now. You're just trying to get through the challenges of the current season of life. But, believe me, the days may drag, but the years fly by. Imagining the next generation in your family might keep you motivated to stay connected with your own kids. Even if they are not pleasant to be around right now.

When your son or daughter becomes a parent, you may be surprised how your role changes and suddenly you have some new and exciting opportunities and responsibilities. Briefly, here's how to secure your place in the hearts and minds of your grandkids.

- Be in their life. Be intentional about scheduling regular time together. It's real easy to go months without any contact. Even if you're two states away, don't go more than a couple weeks without a quick visit, overnight stay, or Skype conversation.

- Start new traditions. From summer trips to the amusement parks to monster truck rallies. From feeding ducks to storytime at the library. Make a checklist of all the cool museums within 50 miles and see them all. Do stuff with your grandkids that slows them down or speeds you up.

- Teach things that their own mom or dad either over-looked or never took the time to teach them. How to fill out a baseball scorecard. How to juggle. How to play crib-bage, canasta, hearts, or chess. How to use a jigsaw safely. How to tie a necktie. Origami. Croquet. Hopscotch. How to use a compass, build a campfire, or find the North Star. How to eat with chopsticks. How to blow a bubble-gum bubble. When their parents are surprised by that new talent, your grandchild will simply say, "It's something Grandpa taught me."

- Identify a special place you can talk and dream with them. A workshop, garden, home office, porch swing.

- Instead of buying a red Corvette when you turn 60, buy a minivan with seat belts for all your grandkids. It's espe-cially valuable when you go on an adventure with grand-kids from different families. Sometimes the only time cousins see each other is when grandparents orchestrate an activity for all of them.

- Tell them how God has worked in your life.

One of the most important things a great dad can do is lay the groundwork to be a great gramps.

101

Teach Them How to Love.
And How to Be Loved.

Everyone who loves has been born of God and knows God.
Whoever does not love does not know God, because God is love.

1 JOHN 4:7-8

If you've been paying attention at all, you will have realized that being a great dad is all about loving your kids. In many ways, that takes time, creativity, intentionality, and patience.

From holding them as newborns to catching fireflies to helping them move into their own place someday. From quitting smoking to insisting they put down their phones to rescuing them at the top of any slippery slope. Snuggling, chatting, apologizing, forgiving, splurging, and exploring.

Do these things (and more), and you're well on your way to teaching and modeling love to your kids.

But the lesson can't just stop with *acts* of love. Your kids need to know the *source* of love. They need to know how the Creator designed each of us to love, but that's only possible if God has changed our hearts through grace.

Only after you accept God's love, can you finally fully love your children. What's more, when you consider how much love you have for your children, you get just a glimpse of how much God loves you.

Love is the greatest command. That God loves you is the truest thing about you. Love is the easiest thing to acquire. And yet sometimes the hardest thing to accept.

It's tragic how many children grow up feeling unlovable. Some people spend their entire lives trying to earn love without realizing they already have the unconditional love of the Creator of the universe.

- "God demonstrates his own love for us in this: While we were still sinners, Christ died for us" (Romans 5:8).

- "God so loved the world that he gave his one and only Son, that whoever believes in him shall not perish but have eternal life" (John 3:16).

- "Love bears all things, believes all things, hopes all things, endures all things" (1 Corinthians 13:7 ESV).

That's right. God knows everything about you and your children and loves you in spite of all those sins and shortcomings. God's love made you. God's love prepared a place in eternity for you. And God's love put Jesus on the cross to pay the price for the sins of every man, woman, and child who puts their faith and trust in him.

He even has a wonderful plan for you and your family and has given you specific gifts, experiences, and talents to make that plan come true. Helping your kids accept God's love is the most important thing a dad can do.

Notes

1. Joe Carter, "9 Things You Should Know About Prayer in the Bible," *The Gospel Coalition*, May 5, 2014, http://www.thegospelcoalition.org/article/9-things-you-should-know-about-prayer-in-the-bible.

2. Brian D'Onofrio, "Divorce begets divorce—but not genetically," *Indiana University News Room*, July 10, 2007, http://newsinfo.iu.edu/news/page/normal/5982.html.

3. Sara McLanahan and Gary Sandefur, *Growing Up with a Single Parent: What Hurts, What Helps* (Cambridge, MA: Harvard University Press, 1994).

4. Deborah A. Dawson, "Family Structure and Children's Health and Well-being: Data from the National Health Interview Survey on Child Health," *Journal of Marriage and the Family* 53 (1991): 573-84.

5. Peter Hill, "Recent Advances in Selected Aspects of Adolescent Development," *Journal of Child Psychology and Psychiatry* 34 (January 1993): 69-99.

6. Wade Horn and Andrew Bush, "Fathers, Marriage, and Welfare Reform," *Hudson Institute* Executive Briefing (Indianapolis, IN: Hudson Institute, 1997).

7. Mark Lino, Kevin Kuczynski, Nestor Rodriguez, and TusaRebecca Schap, "Expenditures on Children by Families, 2015," Miscellaneous Report No. 1528-2015, US Department of Agriculture, Center for Nutrition Policy and Promotion, revised March 2017, https://www.cnpp.usda.gov/sites/default/files/expenditures_on_children_by_families/crc2015.pdf.

About the Author

Prior to becoming a full-time author and national speaker, **Jay Payleitner** served as a freelance radio producer for a wide range of movements and ministry leaders including Josh McDowell, Chuck Colson, The Salvation Army, Bible League, Voice of the Martyrs, and National Center for Fathering.

As a family advocate, life pundit, and humorist, Jay has sold more than a half-million books, including *52 Things Kids Need from a Dad*, *Quick Tips for Busy Families*, and *What If God Wrote Your Bucket List?*

As a national speaker, Jay engages audiences at men's events, marriage retreats, fund-raisers, writers' conferences, and creative training sessions. He has spoken at Moody Bible Institute's Pastors Conference and Iron Sharpens Iron conferences in ten states. Jay also served as executive director of the Illinois Fatherhood Initiative and testified in Washington, DC, at a summit on Responsible Fathering.

Jay and his high-school sweetheart, Rita, live in the Chicago area, where they raised five awesome kids, loved on ten foster babies, and are cherishing grandparenthood. There's much more at jaypayleitner.com.

More great books on family relationships by Jay Payleitner

52 Things Kids Need from a Dad

365 Ways to Say I Love You to Your Kids

52 Things Wives Need from Their Husbands

One-Minute Devotions for Dads

52 Things Daughters Need from Their Dads

52 Things Husbands Need from Their Wives

52 Things Sons Need from Their Dads

10 Conversations Dads Need to Have with Their Kids

52 Things to Pray for Your Kids

The Dad Book

It's Great Being a Dad
(with Carey Casey and Brock Griffin)

52 Ways to Connect as a Couple

The Dad Manifesto

Quick Tips for Busy Families

The Little Book of Big Ideas for Dads and Daughters

To learn more about Harvest House books and
to read sample chapters, visit our website:

www.harvesthousepublishers.com

HARVEST HOUSE PUBLISHERS
EUGENE, OREGON